*

Climbing the Blue Mountain

Climbing the Blue Mountain

TAKE THE NEXT STEP ON

YOUR SPIRITUAL JOURNEY

EKNATH EASWARAN

 NILGIRI PRESS

First published as The Supreme Ambition.
Third edition 2022.

I S B N : 978–1–58638–149–3 (paperback)
I S B N : 978–1–58638–151–6 (hardcover)
I S B N : 978–1–58638–070–0 (ebook)

Cataloging-in-Publication Data

Easwaran, Eknath
  Climbing the blue mountain : a guide for the spiritual journey /
by Eknath Easwaran. – 2nd ed.

    p. cm.

  The essays in this book appeared originally in The little lamp, from
1964–1992.

    ISBN 0–915132–70–2 (pbk.: alk. paper)

    1. Spiritual life.   I. Title.
BL624.E15 1992
294,5′44—dc20   92–10306   CIP

Nilgiri Press is the publishing division of the
Blue Mountain Center of Meditation, a nonprofit
organization founded by Eknath Easwaran in 1961.

www.bmcm.org | info@bmcm.org

The Blue Mountain Center of Meditation
Box 256, Tomales, California 94971
Telephone: +1 707 878 2369 | 800 475 2369

Table of Contents

Preface

THE FIFTEEN ARTICLES in this collection are a call to a higher state of consciousness than we experience in our normal waking moments. This supreme state is the goal of life. Every great scripture has described this goal and given directions for reaching it. Yet most of us dawdle along the way, getting absorbed in passing fancies.

Since 1960, in literally thousands of informal talks, Eknath Easwaran has been teaching people in this country how to reach this goal. Many in his audience have been coming for years, for these talks fill a deep human need: practical, universal, thoroughly enjoyable.

Over the years some of the best of Eknath Easwaran's talks have been edited and published in a quarterly journal, *The Little Lamp*. From the liveliest has come this book. Its pieces can be read separately, but a strong thread runs through them all. From an invitation to "take the plunge" they lead us through the world of the mind to journey's end, Self-realization.

"God does not reserve such a lofty vocation for certain souls only," says John of the Cross. "On the contrary, he is willing that all shall embrace it. But he finds few who permit him to work such sublime things for them." This book is by one who has become aware of "such sublime things" and urges his readers to aspire to the same awareness by following simple, age-old directions.

– THE EDITORS

Introduction

SOMETIMES I USED to go to travel agencies such as Thomas Cook & Sons or American Express just to sit in a chair and watch what went on. They have all kinds of intriguing pictures on the walls to tempt people. Right in front of you, at eye level, a sun is setting in an orange blaze of glory in the sea beyond Bombay. People would come in and gaze. "Peter," a lady will exclaim, "we've got to see that!"

Peter says quietly, "Yes, honey."

He doesn't dare say what he really thinks: "It's the same old sun that sets in the lake behind Buffalo!" Most people forget that the sun sets right here at home too.

"Let's just ask," his wife says. "It doesn't cost anything to ask."

They stand at the counter and their eyes fall on brochures in opulent color describing tours and cruises, cunningly arranged like a Japanese fan. The sign invites, "Help Yourself." Very few people can refrain when something is offered free. They pick up as many brochures as they can hold, muttering, "We can pass them on to the children." But on the way home they start reading, and they get interested.

In this book, you can look upon me as a travel agent for the world within. I will be showing you some beautiful posters of spiritual achievement – Sri Ramakrishna, Saint Teresa of Avila, Mahatma Gandhi – and I will be describing some of the most breathtaking inner landscapes. The captions are of a sort you will not find in any other travel agent's brochures: "Here you see rising a sun which will never set."

Whenever I speak or write about such sights, everybody gets interested, because all of us are secretly longing for such adventures. "Where can we see this kind of splendor? Are you talking about Helsinki, in the land of the midnight sun?"

"Not at all," I say. "That's still the same old sun you see in Buffalo." And I recite a marvelous stanza from the eleventh chapter of the Bhagavad Gita:

> If a thousand suns were to rise together,
> The blaze of their light would resemble a little
> The supreme splendor of the Lord within.

That is the glory of the Self within you, within us all, and the journey inwards to find this Self is the greatest adventure known to mankind.

Several years ago, San Francisco hosted an exhibition from Germany called "The Splendors of Dresden," rich with decorative items made of precious metals and encrusted with gems, some dating from Renaissance times. It was a very popular exhibit, because it is easy for us to get attracted to splendors that are outside.

Even more popular was the "Treasures of King Tut" exhibit. People stood in line for hours to see this array of art and artifacts. If I may coin a pun, what they are really looking for is not King Tut but *Tat*, which is Sanskrit for the shining source of love, the Self, in the depths of consciousness. It is because we hardly suspect its presence that we travel around the world looking for external splendor instead of turning inward to find the vast treasures of the spirit locked up within.

The all-important difference is this. At "The Splendors of Dresden" secret eyes both human and electronic watched from behind screens and walls to make sure visitors did not carry away some of the booty. At the exhibition inside, "The Splendors of the Spirit," the call is, "Help yourself to everything you see." You go into the Hall of Forgiveness and pick up all you can carry; when you come out, the hall is still full. You enter the Hall of Wisdom and help yourself; the supply is untouched. Such fullness, such completeness inside, brings with it permanent security and that rarest of gifts: the ability to love everybody without expecting anything in return.

✳

Like any good travel guide, it is only after I have roused your interest in seeing these sights that I sit down with you to discuss terms. First of all, there is a limit on the amount of luggage you can bring with you. If airlines did not have a forty-pound limit, people would want to bring along their motorcycles to save on gas, a small library to keep them occupied while they get a tan, a few favorite plants, and some gymnasium equipment to work off that rich restaurant fare. So the Civil Aeronautics Board has laid down certain restrictions, meant not to discriminate against anyone but to ensure that the plane will be able to get off the ground.

It is the same story with the tour within. Please do not pack your selfish attachments or resentments; there is no room. And if you do not leave your favorite carry-on cravings behind you at the ticket counter, your plane will never get airborne. Everything has to be reduced to the size of two medium suitcases, which for most people is a long, painful process. But if you want to reach what Jesus calls the kingdom of heaven within, you will find you can get along much better without encumbrances.

This is one reason why I find interior travel so satisfying: you actually *can* "get away from it all." If Princess Cruises could offer this, I might be working for them instead of touting for the spiritual life. But that is just the problem: wherever we go to get away from it all, we take along everything we want to get away from.

Recently my wife and I saw an Indian movie in which the happy couple goes off to Malaysia. While they enjoy the sights, they sing an interminable song about "joyful Singapore." It might indeed be joyful, except that there at the airport to meet your plane will be a color guard of all your old problems, with a song guaranteed to spoil your fun: "Welcome, welcome! What would we do without you, and what were you planning to get away with that did not include us?"

Not so when you know how to travel the world within. When you meditate deeply (for instructions see page 127), it is like taking off in a plane to which your resentments, cravings, and problems have no tickets. As you taxi down the runway, you can see them clustered at the airport window, waving and calling you back: "Wait! Come back! You'll be sorry!" But you are intent on reaching your destination, and with determination you set your eyes on the sky and take off.

When you return, the scene is much different. Most of the resentments have given you up and gone home. The cravings are quiet and friendly and healthy again: "Who needs a cigarette? Let's have a nice run in the park!" And best of all, as you walk down the ramp, your arms are loaded with forgiveness and compassion, and your suitcases are packed with patience and creativity.

This is, as far as I know, the only way to get a real vacation. Worrying about your problems all the time makes for misery with a capital M. For getting away from misery, I recommend the "economy plan," to which I refer throughout this book: do not feed your problems, your ego, with your attention. If you do not feed them, they will slowly lose weight. It makes sense. When we feed them, constantly begging them to have one more helping of attention even when they are gorged, we acquire obese problems that hug us tightly and weigh us down.

So if you really want a vacation, do not think about yourself or brood on your troubles. Do not let yourself get jealous or say uncharitable things about anyone. In other words, do not give the ego breakfast in bed, do not pack it a bag lunch, do not fix its dinner, do not give it pocket money for buying snacks, do not even give it a glass of water. Slowly, surely, the ego will lose weight, until one fine day it will be nothing but a phantom of its former selfish self. You will be able to see right through it.

Recently some distinguished social scientists questioned a large number of people from all walks of life about how happy or unhappy they were and why. Two very interesting results emerged. First, most of the people who described themselves as happy did not attach much importance to money. They did not attach undue importance to pleasure, even sex. And significantly enough, even among those with chronic physical complaints, a good number described themselves as reasonably happy.

"We don't know precisely what makes for happiness," the researchers concluded frankly, "but we hazard the guess that some people have a talent for being happy." The mystics reach a similar conclusion but state it with more precision. Those who often forget themselves in remembering the needs of those around them are happy. Their egos are small, so they find it easy to travel inwards and bring up treasures from the endless splendor within. Meditation and its related disciplines are really a "package plan," whose aim is to pare down our ego-luggage and open up the rich lands inside.

*

I must confess that I do enjoy seeing how people live in other lands. But today I am a chairborne traveler. One evening not long ago, for example, I went with friends to see a travelogue on France. I was pleasantly surprised to find that even though thirty years have gone by since I was there, some vivid memories are still with me. I was able to recognize many of the streets where I did a lot of walking – the best way I know to get acquainted with a beautiful city. But what interests me most of all is people. Buildings, museums, even the Louvre and the colorful Seine are secondary. So naturally I spent the greater part of my time watching people – from sidewalk cafés, in the parks, on the streets, everywhere. What I saw clearly was that there is hardly any difference between the people I grew up with in India and these people of Paris.

I must have devoted a good half of my week in Paris to walking in parks, mostly so I could watch the hundreds of children playing there. I am so fond of children that I have a tendency to see them as my own. After watching these little ones romping about, smiling at each other, crying, quarreling, I realized they were exactly like the brown children I used to see doing the same things in my village.

Next the film showed some lovely beach scenes. I am quite partial to beaches. I had heard so much about the south of France – Nice, the Promenade Anglais, the resorts of Monte Carlo – that I watched with interest and attention. What I noticed was a lot of sharp pebbles, not at all like the soft sands we take for granted in California.

Though it is not on any tourist itinerary, our beach is very satisfying for me. The sand is perfect for walking, and the sea gulls, sandpipers, and sea lions who bask offshore are my old friends. As I watched the movie I said to myself, "Our beach is as beautiful as any of those beaches in France."

Next came beautiful shots of the French countryside, with sheep, lambs, and dairy cows grazing along rolling hills. "What an enchanting sight!" the commentator exclaimed. I had to agree. But I see the same thing every day from my window. After all these enticing sights, I had to conclude, "This is exactly like the place where I live!" What is the difference? Why travel thousands of miles to see sheep and lambs, watch children play in parks, and lie on a pebbly beach?

Suddenly, with profound satisfaction, I realized that right here – wherever I am – is where I am most at home. I have no desire to go somewhere else to see beauty or find happiness; the source of all these is right within. Wherever I live I find beauty, joy, love, and unity.

This is the great realization that comes to all those who have become at home in the world within. No external novelty is needed; when you travel within, every day is fresh with discoveries and challenges, inspiration and profound peace. The scenes I paint for you in the following pages are but a fleeting glimpse of the continuing adventure that awaits you as you enter this world.

Taking the Plunge

A FEW YEARS ago I saw a documentary about penguins, which depicted the lives of these droll creatures almost from the first moment. They looked so human that I found it easy to identify with them as they grew into adults, impeccably attired in evening coats and tails, and set about learning to live in the world around them.

To me it seemed a most inhospitable environment. Penguins hatch in craggy Antarctic rookeries high above frigid waters, which are probably covered with ice for half the year. But the little ones evidently felt quite cozy in those precarious nests. For some time, while they are protected by their parents, they eat, sleep, and do precious little else.

But once the young birds begin to molt, their parents make a drastic move. Up to this time they have been loyal and attentive, inspiring examples for the rest of the avian world. But when it comes time for the children to grow up, the parents simply walk out. There is a great parade of them away from the rookery, and the scene they leave behind is sorrowful indeed. The fledglings I saw looked so dazed that I had to keep reminding myself it was all part of a larger picture. Unless the parents leave them, the children will sit in the nest and never grow up, having their five meals a day, quarreling over who gets what, and never learning to fend for themselves.

With their parents gone, the children naturally began to feel hungry. One day passed; they suppressed their hunger. Two days passed, and their stomachs grew insistent. Finally, after three days or so, they could stand it no longer. Some of them ventured out of their nests.

Penguins are inquisitive by nature, and one of the fledglings in this film was more inquisitive and daring than any of the others. I called him Peter, and he really captured my imagination. I could almost see what was going on behind those curious, beady eyes as he waddled to the edge of the cliff and peered down at the cold, gray waves crashing against the rocks below. Instinctively he must have known that the sea meant fulfillment. If he could only get into the water, he would not die on the rocks but live as a penguin should. But his senses were telling him just the opposite. He hurried back and told the others, "This is death! Better to stay here and go hungry than to face such a terrible fate."

The rest of the rookery were all too willing to agree. "This may not be much of a life," their faces said, "but it's better than violent death. Who knows? Mom and Pop may still come back."

But Mom and Pop did not come back, and finally the hunger grew so fierce that they could not live with it any longer. One morning Peter made his way slowly back to the edge of the cliff. He was still afraid, but anything must have seemed better to him than starvation. He closed his eyes and, with one brave leap, he hurled himself out into the air. The expression on his face said clearly, "My number is up!" We heard a great splash; I could almost feel the shock of the icy waters. Peter disappeared beneath the waves.

There was an agonizing pause. Then, to my great relief, up bobbed a bright-eyed, slightly sheepish little face. Peter churned with his wings and waggled his tail vigorously. Within minutes he was swimming gracefully through the waves, at home at last. "Hey," he squawked up to his friends. "Come on down! This is what we were born for."

Some of the other penguins waddled to the ledge and poked their heads over to see. But even after seeing Peter's exuberance, only two or three were willing to take the plunge. Most of them decided to approach their destiny by stages – that is, they hunted for ledges by which they could walk down. They took a lot of time about it too, looking for just the right ledge and then descending with excruciating care. Only after they were perched about six feet above the water would they cautiously fall in. But once they were in, they too began to crow. "Hey, Pete, wait up! You were right; this is really living."

Still some were not prepared to take this last little six-foot plunge. They just sat there on the lowest ledge, and no amount of frolicking on the part of their friends could induce them to dive in. But even for them, all was not lost. Gradually the tide rose, and one by one the waves washed every penguin into the sea.

I found this a very heartening ending. The whole of life, the mystics of all religions tell us, is moving inexorably toward the sea of joy and fulfillment that we call God. Some – great saints like Teresa of Avila or Mahatma Gandhi – plunge into this sea boldly. Many of the rest of us, busy with other pursuits, wait for the tide to rise. But none of us is lost. Life *has* a goal, and in the Hindu and Buddhist perspective, even if it takes hundreds of lifetimes, evolution itself will carry us to the fulfillment of life's purpose, which is Self-realization.

On the other hand, even though we cannot be lost, we can surely dally. Here we have a uniquely human choice: shall we wait for millions of years, knocked about in the painful process of evolution, until we finally enter this sea of joy; or shall we try to enter now, in this very lifetime, by taking our personal evolution into our own hands? Whatever our past, whatever our condition, this is something that can be done by every one of us through the practice of meditation.

Thirty years ago, when I first began to present meditation in talks throughout the San Francisco Bay Area, the subject was looked upon with suspicion. One hard-headed businessman from the Kaiser Corporation gave me his perspective with executive clarity. "Don't talk to me about joy," he said. "Don't tell me about saints or scriptures. If I take the plunge and start practicing this 'meditation,' I want you to tell me just what benefits it will bring me: one, two, three." That struck me as a practical request, so I began to tick them off for him systematically, just as he had asked: one, two, three.

Before repeating my list, however, I should make it clear that when I say "this is what meditation can do," I do not mean meditation alone. Meditation is an immensely powerful internal tool, but to bring its benefits fully into everyday life it must be part of a whole way of living, a complete complement of spiritual disciplines which I present later in this book. (See page 127.)

First and foremost, meditation places the loftiest of goals before us and gives us the means by which that goal can be achieved. No matter how far technology advances, without an overriding goal in life it is not possible to live well, just as without a destination it is not possible to get where you want to go. With a goal, even if you wander, you always know how to regain your course; without a goal, you never even know where you are.

I had a friend in India who once got so restless that he went down to Madras Central, laid his money on the counter, and said. "Give me a ticket."

The clerk, who was used to all kinds of people, asked politely, "Where to, sir?"

My friend shrugged. "Just give me a ticket – any ticket. I don't care where I go."

This seems to be our condition today, and as a result we find ourselves with an increasing number of problems. To make wise choices in life, even in simple matters, we have to have a goal to which we can refer every day. Otherwise events are irrelevant; they do not hang together in any meaningful pattern.

I came across a good illustration of this the other day when I went into the living room and found that our friend Rama had spread the pieces of a jigsaw puzzle all over the floor. "It's an elephant," Rama announced. "But I can't even find a tusk."

I grew up with elephants, so I would have sworn that I could recognize one from every imaginable angle. But nothing on the floor looked like any part of an elephant I had seen.

Then Rama tactfully showed me the picture on the box. "Oh!" I said. "Now I know what I am supposed to be looking for. This must be the trunk; that must be an ear." After that, though it probably would have taken me several hours, I knew I could find all the pieces and put them together if I tried.

This is what meditation enables us to do. In meditation we take an inspiring ideal like the Prayer of Saint Francis of Assisi and set it before us morning and evening: "Lord, make me an instrument of thy peace. Where there is hatred, let me sow love. . . ." An ideal like this gives us a picture to keep our eyes on throughout the choices of the day, so that little by little we can rearrange the pieces of our lives.

As we learn to do this, boredom disappears. Many serious contemporary problems can be traced back to acute boredom, which is intimately connected with lack of purpose. Once you are practicing meditation sincerely and systematically, every moment opens up choices. Every morning you wake up knowing that you can give a good account of yourself and make a contribution to the welfare of people around you. You do not have to ask whether the day is going to be pleasant or whether you will get your way. You expect difficulties, yet you know you have the capacity to overcome them too. In this kind of confident expectation, where is the room for boredom?

Second, meditation brings vibrant health. Partly this is because it offers an effective way of relieving the stress of life, to which so many physical and emotional problems are due. Banks in India used to have a cardinal rule: until the books were balanced after the day's transactions, no one was allowed to go home. Similarly, we should make it a rule to balance our stress-books every day. Stress accumulates in all of us; that is the nature of life. Trying to avoid problems and challenges means avoiding life itself. But when stress builds up, it has a dangerous effect on health. If you know how to meditate you can sit down for half an hour before going to bed and discharge the stress of that day, so you can fall asleep with a clear ledger. Then in the morning you can sit down for another half an hour or so, to relieve the stress that the busy mind has been accumulating while you sleep.

In addition, meditation brings the understanding and the will to change harmful ways of living. I think it was Dr. Paul Dudley White who observed that when we hear the words "heart attack," it sounds as if the heart is attacking us. Not at all, says Dr. White; the heart is a faithful, sturdy old pump. It is we who attack the heart, and our weapons are not only conventional ones like fatty, salty foods, alcohol, and sedentary living. We have some effective invisible weaponry too: anger, resentment, hostility, impatience, jealousy, competitiveness, worry. Even such diffuse problems as a lack of purpose in life can stage incessant attacks, not only on the heart but on other systems of the body too.

Recently a prominent scientist stated that it is biologically possible for a human being to live one hundred and forty years. Just imagine! Most of us think we are doing well if we make it through half that period. As we creep into our thirties and forties, the machine we call the body naturally begins to develop mechanical problems – some of which are unavoidable, many of which are not. Many of the afflictions we associate with old age, including senility, are not at all inevitable. By drawing on meditation, we can avoid such afflictions by changing our ways of living while we are relatively young.

Finally, even if physical problems do develop, they can often be solved through meditation. Over the years I have seen people with serious physical ailments heal themselves in this manner. Their friends think they have worked a miracle. Such miracles do happen, but as usual with miracles they require a tremendous lot of hard work. I prefer the approach of my grandmother, my spiritual teacher. When I asked her as a boy what she would do in a particularly distressing situation, she would often say honestly, "I wouldn't get myself into that ridiculous situation." It took me a long time to appreciate that kind of answer. But today I can see that meditation's biggest contribution to health is to help us avoid destructive habits of thinking and living, so that we can all come into our legitimate human legacy: long, healthy, hopeful, fulfilling lives.

This brings a sense of fulfillment that nothing else can. Speaking for myself, I have had all the advantages a person can have in India. I come from a well-respected and very loving family, grew up in a beautiful, prosperous village with loyal friends, received my education from excellent, dedicated teachers. Later I had a rewarding career as a writer and professor of English literature. I loved my subject and was deeply devoted to my students – as, if I may say so, they were to me as well. Instead of being paid to teach them, I used to feel I should pay the university for allowing me to share with others some of the finest literature in the world. So when I took to meditation, it was not from frustration or lack of confidence or success. The simple truth is that I began to find even the greatest of life's satisfactions not so very satisfying.

A person in this situation becomes aware of a kind of gnawing hunger deep inside, the sort of hunger one does not know how to satisfy. It can take many forms. One problem that began to torment me at the university was that though I knew how to teach my students about Shakespeare and Spenser, I did not know how to teach them what they most needed and wanted to know – how to live. Because they trusted me, they would often come to me to ask about some of life's basic problems. "I feel terribly jealous," one would say. "What should I do?" And I would not have a real answer. I could quote Shakespeare –

> O beware, my lord, of jealousy;
> It is the green-eyed monster which doth mock
> The meat it feeds on. . . .

But that was all, and it did not really help.

Now, however, after many years of training my mind through meditation, I know just what to suggest. In fact, I have been able to help a good many people help themselves overcome this problem, and the satisfaction that this brings me cannot be gained from any other achievement.

Mahatma Gandhi once said something that appealed to me deeply: It is not possible to be completely happy unless everyone in the world is happy. As meditation deepens, wherever you find sorrow – in the lives of your friends, in a community crisis, even in a tragedy on the other side of the globe – that sorrow is your own. But at the same time, this deeper sensitivity releases the capacity to help. You find ways to help others solve physical problems, set emotional difficulties right, repair their relationships, and even forget their personal problems in making a lasting contribution to the rest of life. In this way the power of sorrow is harnessed, and the deep gnawing hunger I spoke of begins to be relieved.

Jawaharlal Nehru used to say of Gandhi that though his "eyes were often full of laughter . . . yet there were pools of infinite sadness." It is a strange commingling – joy in the unity of life, sorrow wherever this unity is violated. Together these two release determined, selfless, nonviolent action to establish love where there is hatred, trust where there is suspicion, peace where there is war.

＊

One morning last summer I went for an early walk on the beach. The sun was scarcely up, so the air and the water were still quite cold. Yet even at that hour I saw two fellows in black rubber suits sitting on surfboards far offshore, waiting for the waves. Now and then a swell came up and they would ride it – scarcely a wave at all, just a rise in the water a foot or so high. I could tell from the disdainful way they handled their boards that they were disappointed; they wanted bigger surf. It shows how different two attitudes can be. To me a big wave charging down on you is something to run away from. But to them a big wave means danger, adventure, opportunity. When they get good enough, no surf around here will challenge them; they will have to go to Hawaii and take on the huge waves of Waimea Bay.

That is the attitude meditation brings toward personal problems. As your mastery grows, problems that once looked overwhelming begin to shrink to child's play. Then you start to take on some real challenges on behalf of people around you.

Just as in surfing, it takes time and assiduous effort to gain this kind of mastery. Imagine what is required to learn to stand up on an eight-foot piece of fiberglass and weave your way down the face of a pounding, towering wave! With the same kind of effort you can learn to face any challenge and live in such a way that the world benefits from your life.

I admire the daring of young people who master skills like surfing. They have to undergo very dedicated training, perhaps for several years – just as I have had to do in learning to master my life. The main difference is our priorities. For them surfing goes at the top of the list. For me nothing comes before learning how to live. After that, we can take on surfing or skiing or anything else we choose. But unless we know how to live, no matter what else we do know, life itself will slip through our fingers.

When I read about people, especially older people, following the surf to Hawaii or the snow to South America, I remember the haunting lines in the Bhagavad Gita where the Lord says,

> I am come as time, the waster of the peoples,
> Ready for that hour that ripens to their ruin.

Young or old, there isn't much time allotted to us. We should remember this every day. When we see life's supreme goal clearly, we become acutely aware how urgent it is to learn to live. Then we stop saying to ourselves, "Oh, I can afford to wait. One more week, what does it matter? One more month – why not wait till the New Year?" We cannot afford to waste even a minute of our lives; for as Thoreau says, we cannot kill time without injuring eternity.

This sense of urgency itself is one of the greatest benefits of meditation, perhaps even greater than physical health or emotional security. It brings all our activities into focus. Every moment becomes precious, for every moment is an opportunity to move closer to the goal of life.

The Jewel in Our Hearts

I READ IN the newspaper one morning that the largest diamond in modern history, over three hundred fifty carats, had been discovered in one of the big South African mines. Many people who saw that story must have exclaimed to themselves, "If only I could find a diamond like that in my backyard!" It would mean untold wealth, untold prestige.

Yet we already possess the greatest jewel in the history of the world – past, present, and future too. The same figure of speech is used in the Buddhist mantram *Om mani padme hum*: *mani* means jewel, and *padme* here refers to the human heart. All of us have a supreme jewel in the depths of our hearts, and we have come into life for no other purpose than to discover this jewel here on earth while we are alive. But we must be prepared to search for it every day of the week, every week of the year, perhaps for all our life. This search is meditation and its allied disciplines, which can truly be called an adventure in mining the unfathomable depths of human consciousness.

In the days when British interests predominated in India I once visited the Kolar gold mines outside Bangalore, capital of the beautiful state of Mysore. When I got out of the train all I could see was mountains of rubble, not a very pleasing spectacle. But the man accompanying me explained that this was what had been dug out of the earth through arduous labor over many years, until finally a railway track could be laid into the heart of the mines. Those mountains of rock and dirt were monuments to the effort it had taken to hollow out the solid rock. But now anyone who chose to could travel into the mines in comfort and look about, just as we proceeded to do.

In other words, we cannot expect diamonds to be lying around in our backyard. We do not go out to plant tomatoes, lean on our shovel, and bring up the Koh-i-noor diamond: if we find anything that way, it has to be some plastic imitation. To get a three-hundred-fifty-carat diamond we have to do a tremendous lot of excavation; otherwise we must settle for a few pebbles that we can pick up on the beach. But once we have the mine dug and the track laid, we can bring up treasure day after day.

Sri Ramakrishna, the spiritual giant of nineteenth-century Bengal, describes meditation in similar language. When you start digging into consciousness, he says, you make tremendous discoveries. "But when you hit a rich vein of copper ore," he might add, "don't stop and gloat over it. Keep on digging."

"What will we hit next?" his students would ask eagerly.

"Well," Sri Ramakrishna says, "how about silver?"

"Silver! Wonderful! We can make Tiffany bracelets and hedge against inflation."

"But don't stop with being silver tycoons. Keep on digging. You may find gold."

"*That's* what we want," exclaim the students. "We'll be rich!"

"What have I been telling you?" Ramakrishna says, a little vexed. "Don't content yourself with mere gold, man. Keep on digging! When you get really deep, you'll bring up three-hundred-carat diamonds."

This is what takes place when you practice meditation regularly and follow the allied disciplines to the very best of your ability. First your health improves; some long-standing physical problems may be alleviated. But don't stop there. In the next stage you will learn to solve difficult emotional problems. If you persist, you may make your whole life a work of art, so that not only you but those around you benefit from your patience, understanding, love, and wisdom. Gradually even people who do not like you learn to respond to you, by responding to what is deepest in themselves. Then your life is a lasting contribution to all.

But even this is not enough. After you have solved physical and emotional problems and made your life a creative force, one great achievement remains: the personal discovery that all of us are one and indivisible. This is not a philosophical discovery; it is something you experience in every cell. All feeling of otherness vanishes forever. Wherever you go, in whatever circumstances you find yourself, with whomever you live, you will be able to bridge the gap between individuals, races, and nations. This tremendous discovery is the goal of life. Until we achieve it, whether we make money, become famous, enjoy ourselves, or achieve power over others, there will be a crying vacuum in our hearts – a nagging whisper telling us from deep inside, "You haven't found what you came here to find. You haven't discovered the priceless jewel in your heart."

Sometimes people object, "You're asking me to dedicate my whole life to this discovery? I just don't have the capacity." All of us have this capacity, simply by virtue of our being human. But we fritter it away in a hundred and one little ways.

To take just one example, look at cooking. There is so much interest in it, so much time we invest in it! Meditation requires no more.

I have to confess here that my cooking record is pretty bad. In my ancestral home I was scarcely allowed to make a cup of tea. When I first came to the United States, many years ago, I once put a few things together to treat some friends to what I thought was a sumptuous Indian meal. After that, as John Bunyan would say, I saw them no more. So I am not in a position to talk about the niceties of fine cooking. But I am in a position to state categorically that the practice of meditation requires only the same time, the same application, and the same regularity.

Take regularity first. What is more regular than mealtimes? My grandmother knew how to use this to advantage. Whenever she asked me to attend to some errand on my way back from school and I forgot amid the emergencies of high school life, she would ask me a simple line of questions.

"Did you get that coconut for me to take to the temple?"

"No, Granny."

"What happened?"

"I forgot."

"Little Lamp," she would say, looking me straight in the eye, "did you ever forget to eat your breakfast?"

If you want to be regular about meditation, all you have to do is make a simple rule: no meditation, no breakfast.

In other words, there is nothing miraculous in being regular about meditation. We need only give it the same application that millions of people give to undertakings nowhere near as profitable.

It is the same with dedication. How much attention we lavish on doing things we like! It simply is not accurate to say we lack capacity for dedication. If we only bring together all our faculties for enjoying what appeals to us, our desires will be unified and powerful. We will be able to go into the depths of the mind, seek out the jewel there, and bring it up to be worn daily, beautifying not only ourselves but those around as well.

In Sanskrit, this jewel is called the Atman – literally, the Self. I know of no more perfect name in any language. It introduces no theology, requires no metaphysics: *Atman* means simply that this is who we really are. But the Hindu scriptures go on to describe this Self in the most glowing terms as *satyam shivam sundaram* – unchanging truth, abiding joy, flawless beauty.

Satyam is that which is true or real – literally, that which always is. Looking at our busy attempts to find pleasure here and profit there, the mystics ask, "Isn't this like going to the beach and picking up foam and froth? How long do you think satisfactions like these can last?" Imagine filling a suitcase with seafoam and bringing it home as if it were a treasure. "Ladies and gentlemen, I've got a suitcaseful! You'll all want to see." Open the suitcase and all you see is a wet lining. That is what most selfish pleasures are like. They do appear to satisfy us for the time being, but in the long run they cannot help leaving us desolate in body, mind, and spirit.

Most material satisfactions are like this. While we are young they hold out all sorts of promises, but after the first flush of youth is over, when the first half of life's journey nears completion, most sensitive people look back on their past and ask, "What have I achieved? What have I contributed? What have I bequeathed?" Even after material advances we find ourselves insecure, dissatisfied, and discontented, suspecting that somehow we have missed the boat.

Whenever we try to find satisfaction in things that change, we make ourselves more insecure. This is especially true of the physical body, which virtually all of us believe we are. As time passes, we look in the mirror every morning and say, "Mirror, mirror on the wall, who's the fairest of them all?" The mirror replies coldly, "Not you."

No amount of cosmetic surgery or makeup can stop the work of time. Omar Khayyam says hauntingly,

> The Bird of Time has but a little way to go;
> And lo, the Bird is on the wing.

Even as you are reading this, your body is changing a little with age. Therefore, the mystics say, do not identify with your body or depend upon it for security. Look upon it as your house, your vehicle, and keep it in good condition. Identify yourself with the Self, which does not change, and you will become more and more secure with the passage of time.

The second aspect of the Self is *shivam*, abiding joy. Look around and see how people try to enjoy themselves. Over one long holiday weekend more than five hundred precious lives may be lost on the highways, mostly due to the frantic desire to find happiness somewhere other than where we are, and the state of California in which I live leads the list of casualties. Yosemite Park often seems as crowded as Market Street in San Francisco; Lake Tahoe is like the Financial District at noon. All this rushing about, which leads to such casualties and such sorrow, is a kind of compulsive pursuit, looking outside us in the belief that that is where joy and fulfillment hide.

As long as we cling to this belief, we will never discover the jewel, for the simple reason that we are not even going near the mine. Instead of entering the caverns where this giant diamond was discovered, we stay in our hotel, gazing at plastic models of mines and diamonds in the belief that they are real. Plastic diamonds do shine; they can dazzle your eyes. But a jeweler will say flatly, "Don't waste your time. They're not real." Similarly, the jewel in the heart has little to do with superficial physical attraction. It is *sundaram*: beauty itself, the very source of glory.

Costume jewelry may be cheap, but it is worth no more than it costs. To get real jewels is terribly expensive. Imagine going to the Buddha and telling him, "This 'jewel in the heart' you talk about sounds rather attractive. How much does it cost?" The Buddha would reply, "Everything you have."

Most customers would complain to the Better Business Bureau, "This jeweler has no fixed price! If you ask him how much his jewel costs, he says, 'Everything you have.'" Even those of us who are fairly serious about the spiritual life say, "Blessed One, we understand your offer, but we are not in a position to give you everything. Our love and dedication are tied up in other investments: our condominium, our new personal computer, our stamp collection, our classes in Eskimo cookery. But we'll be glad to give you whatever is left over." The Buddha would reply compassionately, "You'd better keep it for yourself." As the Bible says, "Thou shalt love the Lord thy God with all thy heart, and with all thy soul, and with all thy might." Otherwise, go to another store – one where they have plastic imitations.

But there are a few people who become fascinated by the real jewel. Passing attractions like money, power, pleasure, or fame do not satisfy them. The very best that life can offer – health, security, a long, vigorous, selfless life for making a lasting contribution to those around them – even these are not enough. They set their hearts on what is beyond all change, on joy that never passes, beauty that never fades: in short, on the priceless jewel that is their real Self. They come every day to admire that jewel in meditation. They take photographs of it on the sly, then go back and make little models of it in their daily lives. And they begin to dream about diamonds, huge diamonds like the Koh-i-noor. Finally, after many years of hard work, they come straight to the Lord and say, "All right. We *will* give you everything we have." Then the Lord says approvingly, "The jewel is yours."

Spiritual Wealth

IN THE PAPER I once came across an interesting statistic. There were two hundred thousand millionaires in this country at that time, roughly one millionaire for every twelve hundred people. It is a tribute to American drive.

The mystics have a different way of thinking about wealth. It is not how much we have that makes us rich, they say; it is how much we give – not only of our resources, but especially of ourselves. We may have a basement full of cash or a whole warehouse of possessions; if we are self-centered, we are paupers. Only if we can forget ourselves in giving to others can we say we are truly rich.

According to that article, two hundred thousand millionaires are a good index of the nation's wealth. If only we had two hundred thousand selfless men and women! One for every twelve hundred of the rest of us. Every town would be paradise – as Blake says, "Jerusalem's green land" right here on earth. Such people are lamps that light the paths of everyone. They inspire us to follow their example and make our own contribution every day to the welfare of all.

At least two famous American families are not just millionaires but billionaires: the Mellons of Pennsylvania and the Duponts of Delaware. I am sure many young Horatio Algers have only to read about these dynasties of financial genius for their imagination to catch fire. They will scrutinize their biographies, learn their secrets, and try to imitate them in their lives, all so that they too can someday amass a billion dollars. That is the power of personal example.

But the mystics have their Duponts and Mellons too: men and women like Eckhart, Ruysbroeck, Sri Ramakrishna, Jalaluddin Rumi, Thérèse of Lisieux, and others from every major spiritual tradition of the world. In our own century we have the example of one of the greatest spiritual tycoons the world has seen, Mahatma Gandhi. Gandhi was not some far-off, otherworldly figure. He was a man whom we in India could see, whose words we read in the papers daily; a man with a very ordinary past. Even as a college student I wanted to meet this man and learn his secret. Why did people love and trust him so much? How was he able to disarm virulent, even violent opposition with such grace? It was not enough to read about him; I had to see for myself.

I got down from the train at the railway station at Wardha, the town nearest to Gandhi's ashram. Wardha is almost at the geographical center of India, a kind of symbol Gandhi had chosen in order to show that he was equally accessible to everyone. In the beginning he had been careful to select a remote setting without even a regular road to it, so that he and his friends could carry out their vital work for the country without unnecessary interruptions. But gradually people like me, who wanted to see this zillionaire, started coming without a road. With their feet they made a road, which finally had to be paved and later widened to bear the traffic. Everyone looking for an overriding purpose in life seemed drawn to this little man.

From the station to Gandhi's ashram was a walk of several miles. Even after improvements the road was hot and dusty.

When I arrived I saw a collection of beautiful little cottages that made me think of a beehive; everyone was engrossed in work – spinning, cooking, writing, printing. Yet faces were so cheerful that you would have said all carried their responsibilities very lightly. It was clear that nobody expected payment or even thanks for what he or she was doing. All knew it was a great privilege to be able to work together in this task, which was regenerating not only India but the world as well.

In the evening, after a full day of conferences with people from all over the world, Gandhi emerged from his hut. He didn't look tired or tense, as if he needed a martini. He was so relaxed that my first impression was that he must have been playing bingo the whole day. I said to myself, "That's what I'd like to learn – how to make hard work look like playing bingo." Most of the rest of us make even bingo hard work; some of the people I see pursuing pleasure look so haggard that it must take them until Wednesday morning to recover from a weekend of fun.

The other thing that struck me at Gandhi's ashram was the amity that prevailed. Not only did everyone work in harmony, but after a walk and a simple dinner the whole ashram stayed together for a prayer meeting out-of-doors in the tropical sunset.

Gandhiji sat under a neem tree while representatives of many religions sang hymns. A Buddhist from Japan chanted a prayer and some English Christians sang one or two of Gandhiji's favorite hymns;

he liked "Lead, Kindly Light" and "Abide with Me." Then Gandhi's secretary, Mahadev Desai, began to read aloud the second chapter of the Bhagavad Gita, one of the most memorable pieces of mystical poetry anywhere in the world. The last eighteen verses of this chapter, Gandhi wrote, have "been inscribed on the tablet of my heart." They offer a practical, inspiring portrait of the man or woman who is rich in spiritual wisdom:

> They are forever free who renounce all selfish desires
> And break away from the ego-cage of *I, me,* and *mine*
> To be united with the Lord of Love.
> This is the supreme state. Attain thou this
> And pass from death to immortality.

As I watched, Gandhiji's eyes closed in concentration. His absorption in the verses was so complete that you could almost see the words filling his small frame. Suddenly I understood the answer to the question I had come with. Here was the source of all his wealth – his power, his love, his wisdom, his tireless service. He had turned his back on his little 'I,' his ego; now he lived in all.

In every one of us there is this source of power – unsuspected for the most part, seldom harnessed. When we are pushed and pulled by petty urges, the Gita would say, we are not living to our fullest. We are not using even a small part of the tremendous wealth we have within. Trying to grab things for ourselves closes the door on this vast treasury and locks it tight. Only when we give to the rest of life does it begin to open.

To come and go from this treasury freely, we have to remove every trace of selfish desire from our hearts. Here many good people lose interest. "Give up my desires? No, thanks! My desires are all I've got. Without them, life wouldn't be worth living." They are right. Desire is power, and without the immense power of desire no one can make any progress in the direction of real happiness. What has to go is not desire but *selfish* desire.

In a sense, this is a matter of spiritual engineering. We have to redirect our desires so that their power runs in selfless channels – in other words, to turn purely personal passions into a universal passion for the welfare of all. This is a terribly difficult transformation. But the encouraging part is that when people with strong selfish motives are able to transform their desires, they become dynamos of selfless service. Those with a lot of physical passion, for example, can find a spiritual passion to match.

Look at the lives of the world's foremost spiritual figures. It is not necessarily the man or woman who has always led a respectable life, the person who is satisfied with little, who finds spiritual fulfillment. Often those with a remarkable capacity for causing trouble go far when they get control over their desires. These are people who cannot be satisfied by the usual pleasures, so they resort to raising difficulties all over the place. When at last they are ready to transform their passions, they still have enough vital capital to take them a long, long way.

This too I can illustrate from the financial world. I don't know anything about the Mellons and Duponts; but I am sure that even at the age of six, if a Mellon got a dime, he wouldn't go out and spend it on bubble gum. If you keep spending, how can you amass a billion dollars? Young Mellon would put that dime in his piggy bank and save it, and when the piggy got fat he would take it to the bank where his dimes could earn compound interest.

It is the same with desire. Those who become spiritual millionaires are those who hoard all their little selfish desires. They simply do not spend them, and when selfish desires go unspent they accumulate as vast reserves of selflessness.

Every one of us has many of these little, self-centered desires. They do not look like much, so we do not give them much attention. "Oh, it's just a dime; what does it matter?" It all matters. Everything matters. It is not that ten cents is a lot of money, but spending becomes a habit. We get used to doing what pleases us, and after a while we forget that anybody else has needs. All we can think about is ourselves.

By that time, those little desires have become compulsions. Every big self-centered desire begins as a little desire. Every million-dollar compulsion begins as a ten-cent craving. You just want to go to the store, say, and get two pieces of bubble gum. That's how it starts – something harmless, something small. You want to put something in your mouth; you are standing in front of the grocery store; so you ask your mom to give you change to buy a few pieces of gum. Then, at the movies, you go during intermission to get a small carton of buttered popcorn. Whenever you go to the movies, you have to have your popcorn. Soon you graduate to jumbo-size buckets. And finally it is a packet of cigarettes and a six-pack of beer. Little by little. Everybody who has big, unhealthy desires had them first as little cravings.

In economics, as I recall, there is an Iron Law of Money: "Bad money drives out good." Selfish desires can drive out selflessness too. For those who are not at home with economics – I am one – I can illustrate with a more down-to-earth example, thistles. When we first moved to the country I saw a few small thistles here and there on our hills. I rather liked them. They were heraldic and delicate and reminded me of the stories of Sir Walter Scott which I had enjoyed as a boy; and in addition, they had attractive purple blossoms.

After one or two good rains, however, those thistles appeared less dainty and a lot more numerous. When our neighbors started dropping friendly threats about what might happen if we let our thistles spread to their land, I began to see a thistle as a thistle – in other words, as a menace. They covered the hills and choked out everything else that wanted to grow. It took a long, long time for us to weed them out. Even now we have to be alert and pull them up as soon as they appear, for one thriving thistle can repopulate a hill within a season.

Similarly, the Buddha says, "if you are not watchful, selfish desires will grow in your mind like vines in the jungle. Like a monkey you will jump from tree to tree, never finding fruit – from life to life, never finding peace." Most of us who have lived in villages in India are familiar with monkeys; they are great imitators. If the window is open, they will come and watch quietly while you are shaving. You put the lather on just so, stroke your face just so, and each little monkey watches intently. Then, after you leave for breakfast, one hops up onto the sink, lathers his face just as you did, takes the razor just as you did, and starts right in. The imitation will be perfect – with the difference that when the monkeys leave, they will take the brush and razor with them.

Most of us, the Buddha reminds us, are like these monkeys. We learn through little things. When your child sees you occupying your time with what pleases you, neglecting what you can contribute to him and to others, you are not only making yourself more self-centered, you are teaching him to be self-centered also. This too is an iron law, the law of karma. For better or worse, personal example is a force. The Mellons and Duponts are a force; I have no doubt that they have inspired many others to follow their example. Similarly, if we indulge our personal desires, even if only in little things, it encourages those around us to do the same. Teaching is not just speaking in equations or writing momentous truths on a blackboard. How and what we eat, what we drink, how we talk to people, how we deal with difficulties – all these things influence others deeply, especially children.

In this sense there is a field of forces, selfish and unselfish, swirling around every one of us. You cannot see the field of forces around a magnet, but you can observe its shape by seeing what happens to iron filings when the magnet is brought close. People are very similar. When someone has been indulging his selfish whims for some time, watch what happens when he comes into contact with others. He sits down at the table with a look that says, "Impress me," and everybody wilts. The moment we see such a person coming, we get on guard. "There's Sam!" we think. "He's *always* mean. I'd better get ready to defend myself." It may be unconscious, but as soon as we see a certain somebody coming, all of us raise our shields and stand ready for defense.

This has an inhibiting effect on everyone. Even if you were cheerful before, all that shield-raising sets your teeth on edge. Your arms grow tired. In a word, you get grouchy too – and if you are not careful, you can pass that mood on all day, to your co-workers, your partner, your children, even your dog.

On the other hand, we can choose the way we influence others. If we are patient, thoughtful, and kind, those around us will gradually become more like us. This is much like the effect an audience has on an actor. If you fill the first two rows with frozen faces, even Sir Laurence Olivier will not be able to make Romeo's voice romantic. His talent will be paralyzed; his lines will lack conviction. But let some responsive people sit in front, appreciating every nuance; they will draw out the best he can offer. All his attention will go to them, and his performance will really shine.

This is not such a far-fetched simile. One of the most rewarding parts of my job as a professor was to go to debating competitions and sit right in front, with a few sympathetic colleagues by my side. Up comes Kamala, my favorite student, not used to public speaking but capable of a good performance given the right occasion. The boys in front are wearing expectant smiles: "Imagine Kamala representing our school!" Kamala reads their look and thinks perhaps she had better go back and sit down. Then she catches my eye. My look says, "Come on, Kamala. You know I like your stories. They will too." This is all it takes: somebody whose eyes encourage, whose attitude is eager and unreserved. Kamala launches into her talk, and there is every chance that she will walk away with the prize.

Good, kind, secure people are saying in a thousand little ways, "Come on, Sam! Let's see you try being kind." That is all Sam needs – somebody who knows he can be kind, who appreciates his thoughtfulness at every opportunity. And even if he gets impatient once in a while, he knows there is someone who won't get ruffled or lose faith in him; so he tries again. That is how selflessness spreads.

I would be the first to admit that this is not easy. There are always difficulties: somebody to upset you, someone else to aggravate you, a third to finish the job by sending you home with a headache. That is life. If you complain, "I don't want to get headaches. I'm tired of taking risks," you are going to be lonely all the time. But if you are meditating sincerely, you can learn to be selfless even with the most difficult people. Then you become not only rich but a real philanthropist, distributing wealth wherever you go. It is good to endow a hospital or build a park. But to me the great philanthropists of the world are those like Gandhi, who make their whole lives a gift to the world.

The Forgotten Truth

THE WORD *dharma*, law, comes from the Sanskrit root *dhri*, to support. What supports life, according to the mystics, is the principle of unity; what destroys life is separateness, the negation of this principle.

In compassionate language, the mystics tell us that we have simply forgotten this unity. It is not that we deny it, we have just forgotten. There is a beautiful story narrated in the Hindu tradition which illustrates this point. A young prince is kidnapped by bandits, taken to the forest, and raised there, learning the bandits' life of looting and murder. He completely forgets his princely heritage and all the royal virtues and lives like one of the beasts of the forest, attacking and killing without any feeling of conflict. One day the spiritual teacher from the royal family passes through the forest and recognizes the young man. He has the same features as the king, the same nose, and the same style of walking, but his manner is terribly menacing. So the spiritual teacher, with great love flowing from his heart, approaches the young man and says, "Your royal highness." The young man doesn't understand. He says, "Where is this 'royal highness'?" He expects to be called "you tiger," "you leopard." He has completely forgotten. The spiritual teacher repeats, "I am talking to you, your royal highness." The young man says, "I am not your 'royal highness'; I'm a bandit. Ask me to loot, ask me to kill, I can do it. I'm the Bonnie and Clyde of ancient India." Not repulsed by this picture, and unshaken in his faith in human nature, the spiritual teacher goes up to the young man, puts his arm around him, and begins to tell him stories about his childhood – how his father used to carry him on his shoulders, how his mother used to sing him to sleep, how his life was in the palace. Gradually the prince begins to remember. He says, "Go on, go on!" The spiritual teacher goes on relating anecdotes of his royal childhood. Finally the young man says, "Now I recall. I'm not bad or violent. I simply forgot. You have helped me remember; you are my greatest friend." And the young prince goes home to his father, the king.

*

This is your story and mine. With great simplicity, yet great sophistication, the mystics tell us that we have just forgotten. They say, "You have no love for personal profit." We just smile. They say, "You are not really devoted to personal pleasure." We smile and say, "He doesn't know us." The great mystics say, "You really are not resentful or hostile. You really are not self-willed." And we say, "If it pleases you to say so, we have no objection, but don't say we didn't warn you!" The mystics continue to assure us that one day our eyes are going to be opened, and we will know that we have been dreaming.

If you go to Sproul Plaza tomorrow and tell people that unity is our nature, that love is our nature, that we are hypocrites pretending to be separate, impostors pretending to be selfish, the sophisticated campus crowd will say, "You'd better go home and sleep it off. We know ourselves; we are honest. We know that we are no good and are just wasting our time." The mystics say that this is an illusion, a morbid spell under which we have fallen. This is the meaning of the Sanskrit word *maya*.

Many years ago I read about a powerful magician who had the capacity for mass hypnotism. A performance was announced for eight-thirty. When eight-thirty struck the hall was full, but there was no magician on stage. When nine struck and there was still nobody on stage, people started getting irritable. Finally, when ten struck and there was still no sign of the performer, the audience went berserk, demanding their money back and threatening to burn down the hall. Just then the magician sauntered on stage as if nothing had happened and looked very surprised to see all the angry faces. "Have I offended you in any way?" he asked. A roar came up from the audience: "What does the program say?" He looked at the program and read, "'The performance is to begin at eight-thirty.'" Again a roar came forth. And he said, "Won't you please all look at your watches?" It was only eight-thirty. Then the magician said, "Now I want you all to stand up and apologize." So they all stood up and in one voice said, "We who are gathered here apologize."

Now according to the Hindu tradition, this is what has happened to us. Some magician standing on the cosmic platform says, "Let these people come to believe that they are all separate. Let them come to believe that they are their bodies. Let them come to believe that the voice of the ego is the voice of God." The spell is cast over us, and we all believe that this is our nature. "Honest," we say, "this is how we are." The great mystics in every tradition tell us that we have just forgotten. They repeat stories to wake us up, but most people just do not hear. There is a saying in this country, "It goes in one ear and right out the other." Many people come to my talks, put a couple of dollars in the bowl, sit there for an hour, but do not hear a thing about this. Jesus used to say marvelously that there are none so deaf as those who will not hear. Those who cannot hear can be helped, but there is very little that can be done for those who will not hear, who will not open up their hearts, who will not try to practice spiritual disciplines.

For all of us, however, it still takes many years of listening to the Gita, to the Bible, to the Koran or the Dhammapada before we begin to understand. Finally, somewhere there rings a little bell, just a little tinkle, and we say, "Tell me more." Gradually there is a slight response. We begin to remember our heritage. *Samadhi* according to this interpretation is not union with God but reunion. It is the story of the Prodigal Son replayed in our own consciousness. Remember? The son didn't go to someone else's home. He went to his own father's. And the father didn't say, "Who are you?" He welcomed his son and feasted him. In the same way, the principle of unity is not something new that someone plants in our consciousness. It has always been there, buried fathoms deep and forgotten. The purpose of meditation, then, is to dig down to this unity and recall what has been forgotten.

*

Because this truth is inscribed in the depths of our consciousness, leading a separate life is impossible. Living in harmony with all – our family, our society, all forms of life – is the truth of life, and this truth alone can support us. There are many people who will say that it is human nature to hate, to fight, and to kill, but the mystics say this is the law of beasts. Having become human beings, we have risen above this law. Any human being who hates, who uses violence, who kills, according to the mystics, has gone back to the level of an animal.

In the Dhammapada, the Buddha uses a terrible phrase about people who have reversed their evolution in this way. Those who have forgotten the unity of life and who believe they are separate, who are self-willed and live for their own satisfaction, *natthi papam akariyam,* will not stop at any evil deed. People who are fond of money, for example, begin in a very ordinary way. They don't want to exploit, they don't want to bring about the ruin of other people, they don't want to despoil the land. They simply want to make a certain amount of money, and so they start their business, whatever it may be, in a very quiet way, not too much at the expense of others. But as they get more money their love for money grows. Now, instead of being content with doing a little harm to others, they say, "Why not exploit people? Why not go into massive production of cigarettes, liquor, drugs, or armaments? That will bring us a lot of money." Little by little by little this inordinate love of profit destroys all humanity.

Take, for example, the armament industry. I have been reading recently about Sir Basil Zaharoff, the father of this enterprise. He would go to one country and sell them a particular gun, then go to another country and tell them, "I can sell you a gun which can outshoot that gun." The terrible part of this story is that it is still going on today. With food getting scarcer, and famine stalking across the world, billions of dollars are being spent on armaments. Unfortunately, the highly advanced technological countries are also selling to poor countries, for whom these weapons not only are unnecessary but even displace resources which are needed for providing food.

Such is our confusion that we think, in the language of Sri

Ramakrishna, we have to go east in order to go west. The production and sale of armaments leads to warfare, not to peace. When underdeveloped countries ask for planes and missiles, let us send them wheat and soybeans. This is truly promoting peace. The point here is that those who have engaged in this business of armaments did not start out with hatred; they just wanted to make money. The love of money can gradually make people forget their sense of decency, their sense of kindness, their sense of unity.

One day when I was with my wife, Christine, in San Francisco, we saw two very attractive girls standing on a corner giving away cigarettes in plastic shopping bags. I was amazed to see people who were on the other side of the street crossing over to get those cigarettes. Imagine! Human cupidity is so easy to arouse. This is what the profit-making enterprises bank on. They inflame our cupidity in all kinds of devious ways, and once this happens, we will buy anything. All they have to do is say "more." They don't even have to say more what, we'll buy anything.

A number of years ago I went to a flea market just to see what a flea market was. There was a huge crowd milling around all day. Then about five o'clock, someone in one of the stalls called out over the public address system, "Come to Stall 14. We are giving everything away free." I have never seen a stampede like that. People who were buying things they needed at other stalls dropped everything and rushed to Stall 14 to get something free. They didn't have any idea what it might be, but if it was free, they wanted it.

Every one of us, even if we are not greedy for money, is greedy for pleasure. As long as we are talking about greed for money, there will be a lot of people who will say, "It doesn't apply to me." But who can say that about greed for pleasure? There is even a larger number of people who will line up at a stall if you say: "This is pleasant; you will enjoy this." We will go even if we don't know what it is.

Every one of us has to remember, therefore, that as long as we are driven compulsively by the desire for personal profit and personal pleasure our nature can be vitiated. We will start out, just as everyone starts out, rather nice, maybe sometimes even noble, and on a few rare occasions even selfless. Gradually all these finer qualities wither away and the desire for pleasure and profit changes the look in our eyes and our very life. After a number of years we do not care about other people's needs because we are completely enveloped in what we like, what we enjoy, what appeals to us. It is good to remember that this can happen to anyone.

It is a sad slander on human nature to believe that our very best work can be done only under the compulsion of money or pleasure, but this is what most people believe today. There is a certain amount of work that can be gotten out of people by offering them good wages and overtime, but if you want the best out of people, you have to make a deeper appeal – to their sense of unity. Tell a person that there is no money or pleasure in this, but that he will be contributing toward making his city and his world a better place in which to live, and gradually he will respond. When this appeal gets into a person's consciousness, she gives her very best, joyfully and continuously.

When Mahatma Gandhi wanted people to help in his work, he would give his angelic, toothless smile and say, "I can offer you magnificent rewards: two years in prison, confiscation of all your property, work without respite every day of the week, and the increasing joy of knowing that your life really counts." This is the glory of human nature; the most daring and resourceful people would respond.

It is a basic spiritual law that the person who lives for himself or herself lives in sorrow, while the person who gives freely to all lives in abiding joy. Take the person who lives only for money. I have known a few such people. There was one chap I used to know whose concentration was complete when it came to financial matters: he would see everything in terms of profit or loss. When I would be reading my paper in the morning, he would come and ask me for just one page, the page giving the stock exchange quotations. The rest of the paper did not exist for him – neither news, nor drama, nor sports, nor entertainment. For him the paper meant the stock exchange quotations. And this is the way his memory worked, too. We would say to him, "Do you remember the day Gandhiji passed through town and spoke on the Fort Maidan?" He would say, "Yes, that's the day that Nilgiris Tea went over two hundred rupees." He could tell you the history of the dividend sheets of a particular company for ten years. I had never seen such prodigious recall. But he was completely insecure. He lived in fear that some share would come down, that some company would go broke, or some debtor would leave town. He wasn't a bad fellow, but he was caught in love of money.

There are other people who are misers with time. They say, "I have to go bowling, then I have to do candlemaking, then I have to do some repair work on my motorcycle, then I have to practice my ukelele, and then I have to write some poetry for fortune cookies." These people, too, are misers. Just as the money miser grabs a penny here or there and puts it in his piggy bank, whatever time these people have they must spend in some pleasure. These, too, will never find joy, because they are living for themselves – in violation of the unity of life. In the compassionate language of the mystic, these people are not bad, they are simply immature. They must always play with their toys. Now it is all right for babies to play with their toys, to bite their stuffed reindeer and pull off the ears, but imagine their fathers doing this. Here the mystic would say, "Don't you want to grow up?" He calls us children when we concentrate only on ourselves and completely neglect the welfare of others.

On the other hand, when we live for the welfare of our community, we become healthy and secure. One of the simple secrets the great scriptures give us about avoiding emotional problems is not to think about ourselves, not to dwell upon ourselves, not to brood upon ourselves, but to live for the good of all. It is a simple recipe which we can all practice. Emotional problems like depression, frustration, insecurity, and boredom need come to none of us. If we ask the great mystics why we have these deplorable problems, they will say that we are still children, playing with our toys, lying in our cradles, screaming, "I want this, give me this. I want that, give me that."

*

Now we have all juggled in good measure with our senses and passions, and have found that these things do not bring security or lasting happiness. That being the case, the mystics will ask, "Why don't you try swimming against the current in life?" In my village in Kerala, one of the great pastimes of the boys was swimming in the river, especially when the monsoon flood brought the water over the banks. After an hour of swimming against the current, most of us would end up just a little downstream from where we started. It was considered a mark of great strength for any fellow to make it straight across to the other bank. All the boys built up their muscles in this exercise. The smaller children, on the other hand, would just float with the current, which required little effort or exertion. Similarly, in life most people just float with the current. They don't know anything about the fierce joy of self-conquest.

The Buddha uses a tremendous term to describe this accomplishment, *patisotagami*; those who lead the spiritual life, he says, are "going against the current." It's a phrase which should appeal to the young especially because it is full of challenge. The Buddha tells us: if you want a smooth life, don't follow me, if you want a pleasant life, don't follow me; but if you want thunder, if you want storms, if you want danger and continuing challenges, go against the current. There is a school of thought prevalent today which says that successful living means to flow with life. The Buddha says that successful living is the other way. Flowing with life may bring you money, it may bring a little pleasure, but joy, security, love, wisdom, and unity all lie the other way.

I am not too familiar with the ways of fish, but I understand that the salmon has the rare capacity to swim upstream. It even leaps up waterfalls, I am told. This is exactly what we do in leading the spiritual life. Just imagine leaping over our anger. There it is, coming down like Niagara, and instead of going down in a barrel, we get in a barrel and go up. Even Indiana Jones would be astounded!

But this gives us some sense of the scope of the achievement. When we live this way, every night we will go to bed sore with selfless effort but secure in the knowledge that we have not wasted the day, that we have made some contribution to all those around us. It is this kind of strength that the mystics say is better than pleasure and profit and power, and it can come to all of us when we turn against the current to find our true nature, which is oneness with all life.

The Supreme Ambition

"THERE IS ONLY one thing I want and that is to become a great saint." This an astounding admission from a girl still in her teens: Thérèse Martin, born in France in 1873. Her life was in many ways quite ordinary, even though much of it was lived inside a convent. Yet Pope Pius X called little Thérèse of Lisieux "the greatest saint of modern times." This may seem like a miracle, but in large part it is deep, driving desire pressed into action which brings about the fulfillment of such a sublime ambition.

I have friends who teach in our local high school. Every year they tell me about their school's Career Day, when doctors and airline hostesses, executives and athletes, come to talk to young students about their respective fields. I listen closely, because I like to know what dreams currently capture the imagination of the young. Not once have I heard of a student whose deepest ambition is to become a saint.

There must be a reason for this. I am familiar with a number of very good universities, both in India and in the United States; so I am familiar with their programs, both strengths and weaknesses. I am one of the first to appreciate the good work they do and all the facilities they provide. Yet it strikes me as a woeful lack when I see no attention paid anywhere to what I sometimes call "internal engineering": the training of the mind and senses, so that our passions can be guided and transformed. Very few people even understand the importance of these things; that is why there can be no curriculum. Yet without the magnificent training that enables a person to transform unloving states of mind into loving ones, how can anyone be considered truly educated? It is chiefly a question of priorities. If we are not able to love deeply, whatever our artistic or scientific achievements, we cannot even call ourselves cultured.

Love is a skill, a precious skill that can be learned. In my dictionary, the word "educated" cannot be used to describe any person who is not learning to love, whatever difficulties he or she may have. This does not deny that many other skills are useful, even necessary. But in the end, nothing less than mastering the mind can ever enable us to attain our highest fulfillment.

This is a very compassionate, hopeful outlook, in a day and age when hope is conspicuous by its absence. For from this point of view, the person who is unable to love – who avoids close contact with people, who gets jealous or hostile, who strikes out with sarcastic remarks or ill-intentioned acts – is not wicked; he or she simply has not learned to love. And where do we go to find a curriculum?

The saints of all major religions answer with one voice: while we can draw inspiration from those who practice love in their daily lives, we all have the syllabus of love right inside us, printed on every cell. We need look no further afield. There burns in the recesses of our consciousness a divine spark of pure love, universal, unquenchable. No matter what difficulties we manage to get ourselves and others into in our ignorance, whatever the country we live in or the race we belong to, whether we are rich or poor, learned or ignorant, this spark is never extinguished. It is our greatest glory. From this spark Thérèse's longing for universal love was kindled; from it sprang all her efforts to learn how to bring her love into full flame. It can work the same miracle in each of us.

Then the saints go even further. They tell us that life has only one overriding purpose: to discover this source of infinite love, called in Sanskrit the Atman or Self, and then to express this love in daily living. Without love, life is empty; without love, life is meaningless. The only purpose which can satisfy us completely, fulfill all our desires, and then make our life a gift to the whole world, is the gradual realization of this Self, which throws open the gates of love. We cannot dream what depth and breadth of love we are capable of until we make the discovery that this divine spark lives in every creature.

*

The Upanishads give a precise way to compare the lives of ordinary people to the life of someone aware of the Self. Considering it was made some four thousand or more years ago, it is an amazingly contemporary analysis. Take, they say, a young man or woman, healthy, bright, and highly educated, with a lot of drive and all the material resources required to carry out that drive. Most of us, you know, if we don't have physical problems, have emotional problems. If we don't have either, then we have financial problems. If all these are taken care of for the time being, we lack drive. But this hypothetical personage lacks nothing. "Very lucky fellow," we say. "Very lucky lady."

"Yes," the Upanishads agree, "very lucky. Now take that person's joy as one unit. The joy of the man or woman who is aware of the Self is a million times as great."

Spiritual psychology can rise no higher. When you are enjoying a movie, or apple strudel with whipped cream on top, you might remind yourself that the temporary delight you are experiencing is an infinitesimal reflection of the joy we can have in the Self twenty-four hours a day.

"I do not know what I may appear to the world," said Sir Isaac Newton, "but to myself I seem to have been only like a boy playing on the seashore, and diverting myself in now and then finding a smoother pebble or a prettier stone than ordinary, while the great ocean of truth lay all undiscovered before me." All that most of us have done in life so far is to collect a pebble or two and come home boasting, "Hey, Ed, wouldn't you like to see my collection?" We can multiply our joy a million times by learning to love and live not for ourselves, but for a million other people.

This is just what we do with meditation: learn to expand our love to include more and more people and remember their needs always. This achievement is not superhuman. It is within your reach and mine – within the reach of every human being. Advertisers keep telling us, "Accept no substitutes. Never settle for less." The saints say, "Accept no substitute for the Self. This is the infinite joy you were born for, the infinite love you were born to give."

How do we discover this Self? We can begin humbly by understanding that there is a great deal of self-will in all of us, which expresses itself on almost all possible occasions. Self-will covers our real face; only by getting rid of it can we see who we really are. The other day my friends' little girl, who is one and a half, came to me with mud caked all over her face. Fortunately we all know that mud is not part of a face. We don't say, "Well, you'll just have to learn to live with it." Her mother simply washed it off, and she again looked like a rose in June. Self-will is the same. Even if you have been in the habit of being selfish for a long time, you can soak your face, loosen the habit, and then get a good, heavy washcloth and wash your face until it shines. The saints say, "We have the soap and plenty of wash-cloths too. If you want to wash off your self-will so the Self can shine, we'll help you and show you how."

How do you go about getting rid of self-will? You can't throw it in a Goodwill box! Nobody wants it, I assure you; it's like nuclear waste. Thérèse has a characteristically beautiful solution: we can wash it away by practicing kindness and consideration toward everyone, even if only on a limited local stage.

Thérèse's explanation sounds deceptively simple and mundane. "There are great saints who have won heaven by their works," she says – by great deeds, tremendous acts of sacrifice – "but my favorite patrons are those who stole it. I want to win heaven by a strata-gem of love which will open its gates to me and to all poor people like me." When "great" saints enter heaven, she implies, they go in by the main gate, accompanied by seraphim and cherubim singing carols of praise. But it is not given to you and me to live on such a vast scale. We go round by the tradesman's entrance in the back. If the door is locked, we try the windows; there may be a little crack somewhere through which we can squeeze. And when we're discov-ered, we plead, "Please let me stay! I'm no great saint, but please don't throw me out!"

It is the humility in this wonderful girl that appeals to me so much – the humility and the utter practicality. We all have opportunities to be kind to the people around us, Thérèse reminds us; none of us lacks opportunities. If we strive to maintain an unbroken code of courtesy, consideration, and kindness in the numberless encounters of daily life, we may be able to sneak up on the Self. Even this is far from easy; it requires complete vigilance every day.

Most of us spend years in personal pursuits without ever taking time to know the needs of people in our own home, in our neighborhood, at work. It may be rarely that we give our energy to serving their needs. We should try to remember that the nascent capacity for love we possess is the greatest thing we shall ever have. To nurture it, we should subordinate everything else to loving everyone with whom we come in contact. This means forgetting our petty little adventures in profit and pleasure for their sakes, but that is how love grows. This isn't going to happen early. It takes a lifetime to learn to love. Love does not burst forth one morning with a display of fireworks in the depths of meditation. It grows little by little every day, by bearing with people, as Shakespeare's sonnet says, "even to the edge of doom." That is what love requires. But if only we make it our number one priority, as young Thérèse did, no matter what difficulties come in our way, our love cannot help but grow.

*

When you first feel drawn to someone you find attractive, don't you start sending flowers, lavish more attention on your appearance, refine and soften your language? Similarly, when you begin to feel drawn to the Self, the very source of love, many changes take place in your personality. An inevitable, inescapable transformation begins, which in European mysticism is called the purification of the soul. Your desires and longings become focused more and more on the Self, usually through the inspiration of someone in whom you can see its beauty manifested. For Thérèse, this inspiration was the personality of Jesus. The deep longing to be like the one we love gives us motivation to make great changes in ourselves – many of which are distressing – not only with courage but with a fierce sense of joy.

"How could I love Jesus," Thérèse exclaims, "if I behaved otherwise towards those who hurt me?" If we behave unkindly, she is saying, we don't stand a chance to get close to him. He won't even look at us. Didn't he say clearly, "Inasmuch as ye have done it unto one of the least of these my brethren, ye have done it unto me"? Jesus did not spare words; if we want to love him and to be like him, we must learn to love him in everyone. From this we get motivation to give our time, our resources, our energy to solving the problems all of us face in these troubled times. It is not just a matter of helping our own family, not just a matter of whom we like or dislike. However faintly, we begin to see the Self in everybody. We begin to give to everybody, not for any personal return but for the sheer joy of giving. These are signs that the great day is approaching when we shall see the glory of the Self face to face.

As we near this vision, we feel a great surge of love drawing us onward – "love," says the Christian hymn, "that will not let us go." It possesses and floods our hearts. "One that knows this vision," exclaims Plotinus,

> with what passion of love shall he be seized! With what pang
> of desire, what longing to be one with the object of his love!
> This Beauty supreme, the absolute and the primal, fashions
> its lovers to beauty and makes them also worthy of love.

After this experience, even if we want to, we cannot think about ourselves or pursue private satisfactions; our love will not allow us. As the Hindu scriptures describe it, the Lord becomes a sea of love extending through the entire universe, calling us incessantly: "Strip yourselves of your self-will and come, plunge into Me."

Being always in love is no impossible dream. Everyone can discover the source of love, which means learning to love all. This is just what we are in direst need of today, for loving everybody makes anger impossible, jealousy impossible, violence impossible, war impossible. We say, "It can't be done!" I would answer simply, I have met quite ordinary people who have discovered this source of love within themselves and given it to the whole world. One of them is Mahatma Gandhi, who started out just like anybody else – petty, self-centered, ineffectual. Through practicing love day in and day out, he made his life a gift of love to everybody on earth. The bequest of such people goes on and on, without end in either the near or the distant future.

When your heart is full of love for all, you live in abiding joy right where you are. You have found heaven on earth, as Thérèse found it in her little convent; you can go anywhere and carry heaven with you. If you fly to Europe, when the customs official at Orly airport asks if you have anything to declare, you can say, "Abiding joy." "I'm glad you brought it along," he will probably reply. "We could use some of that here." In other words, if you are in love all the time, you are on holiday all the time – holiday from your own problems. You'll find that when you spend your time helping others to solve their problems, your own will fade away. You won't have time for brooding on yourself, which is the cause of most of our personal problems, because you will always be thinking of ways to give. Then, like Gandhi and Thérèse, you become a beneficial force in life – a force that never dies.

Chasing Rainbows

I AM SITTING in my chair at home in the country, looking out on the green hills. There is everything right here to satisfy me: birds, flowers, animals, trees, reasonable comfort, loyal companions, and the precious opportunity of selfless service. Right here is everything I need for complete happiness always. But as I look out of my cottage window I see a camper in the distance traveling along the road. Somewhere in my mind is the uneasy stirring of a desire to jump on that camper and go out chasing rainbows, to find the pot of gold at the end. This belief that somewhere *out there* is the land of joy dogs our footsteps wherever we go. As long as we look upon joy as something outside us, we shall never be able to find it. Wherever we go it will still be beyond our reach, because "out there" can never be "in here." On the other hand, if I can find joy here and now within myself, I shall of course have it everywhere, under all circumstances. This is what Jesus means when he says, "The kingdom of heaven is within."

Objects of desire depend on what is "in here," within us, for their value. As long as I have a desire for chocolate cake, it gives me some pleasure. When I lose the desire, chocolate cake loses its appeal for me. I can have it right on the table in front of my eyes; as far as I am concerned, it has ceased to exist. What gives value to any object of desire is the desire itself.

When a boy meets a girl and holds her hand for the first time, he expects the thrill to last forever. One year later the touch of the same girl means nothing. When attraction is physical, it does not take long for the desire to fade and disappear. Then the boy thinks that the touch of another girl will bring him lasting happiness – only to be disillusioned again. This can only repeat itself over and over. The trouble is neither with the girl nor the boy; it is the nature of desire to pass.

The mind may be described as an endless series of desires. One desire rises, is satisfied, and disappears, to be followed by another and another and another. It is the nature of the mind to desire, and the nature of desire to change. Any attempt to find an abiding state of joy by satisfying desires, therefore, is doomed to fail.

As long as I desire a yacht, for example, I believe I will find lasting happiness by sailing on it. There is, of course, a certain satisfaction in owning one's own yacht and sailing into the Caribbean. But this satisfaction can last only as long as the desire lasts. As the desire begins to subside – as it must – the satisfaction also begins to diminish. When the desire disappears at last, in the place of satisfaction, boredom sets in.

There is nothing wrong with desire. Like electricity, which can light a home or electrocute the tenant, desire is neither good nor bad.

It is the most powerful force we have to drive us to action. Tragedy comes when desire is not subject either to the intellect or to the conscious will. Then we have a powerful vehicle speeding without anybody in the driver's seat. Imagine all the cars in your home town coming out of their garages and going about anywhere they like without drivers. How many accidents there would be, how much damage to life and property! The same thing takes place among nations, races, families, and individuals, when we pursue our personal desires. I go after what I desire, you do the same, and sooner or later we collide.

*

The vast majority of human beings spend their lives in the pursuit of money and material possessions, pleasure and prestige. These are fleeting goals that burst like bubbles when we pick them up. The man who is trying to make a million dollars, for example, is more a victim of his desire than its master. His eyes are so fixed on his own profit that he often is not aware of the welfare of others.

The fine arts too have their limitations. They may give delight to many, but as long as an artist is ego-centered he cannot perceive the whole. He is confined to his own individuality as limited by the senses – the eye or ear.

Scientists too are limited by the prison of duality. They sit "here" and study stars or bacteria "out there." The most powerful intellect is still a limited instrument, which cannot help cutting things into parts. It ignores the living whole in which the parts act and react on one another continuously.

In order to see life as one indivisible whole, we have to shed all desires for personal pleasure, profit, prestige, and power. As long as these motivate us, we look at life through our individual conditioning. We see life not as it is, but as conditioned by our desires. I can

know you fully only if I *am* you, and that can never be as long as I am
I. To know anyone or anything fully, I must shed what I have come
to believe is my personality – to use the precise Sanskrit word, *aham-
kara*, that which makes me "I," separate from the rest of the world.

This is what Mahatma Gandhi meant when he said that his greatest ambition was to reduce himself to zero. I know of no great artist
or scientist with this ambition. When Gandhi succeeded in reducing
himself to zero through many, many years of spiritual discipline, he
saw life as an indivisible whole in which any injury done to the tini-
est part is injury to all. This realization of the unity of life made him
abjure violence, showing convincingly that nonviolence or *ahimsa* is
the greatest force upon the face of the earth to bring together nations,
races, and families in love and service.

We should never forget this vital distinction between the cultural
contribution of the great artist and the spiritual contribution of the
great mystic. To me the twentieth century is not the space age but
the Gandhian age, because it was Gandhi who showed us in these
times how to live in harmony with the eternal law that all life is one.
This he did not by painting pictures or composing songs on the unity
of life or by traveling to the moon, however valuable these may be,
but by facing without violence some of the most threatening problems of our age.

Of course, civilization has been enriched greatly by artists, scientists, and statesmen of genius. But it is great mystics who bring it
back to its right course and give us through their own life an inspiring glimpse of the shining goal towards which all creation moves
through trial and error. Gandhi has shed his mortal body, but his
immortal spirit, the Atman, can be experienced wherever people
turn away from violence.

One of my friends was warned by an acquaintance not to let meditation turn her into a zombie. I hear this from many people who are afraid they might lose their personality if they eliminate the sense of *I, me,* and *mine* from their consciousness. I remind them that the word "personality" is related to the Latin word *persona,* a mask. In Alexander Dumas's novel, the supposed twin brother of Louis XIV was forced to wear an iron mask for so many years that it became part of him. However hard he tried, he could not take it off to reveal his real face. All of us are like this. Through many years – or many lives – our minds have developed habits of selfishness and separateness through endless efforts to satisfy desires for personal pleasure and profit, power and prestige. If we can throw away this mask of separateness, our real personality, the Atman, shines forth in beauty, wisdom, and love.

Without personal desires, some people ask, how can there be any motivation for action? The best answer to this question too is the life of Gandhi. As long as he was playing games with his personality, young Gandhi was content to spend his days in London eating his barrister dinners, practicing the violin, and trying to learn the fox-trot. But later on in South Africa, when he turned his back on personal pleasure and profit so he could serve the thousands of cruelly exploited Indian laborers there, Gandhi found immense inner resources of which he had never dreamed. While living to satisfy his private desires, he had no access to this treasury of love, wisdom, courage, and inspired action. But once he renounced the petty, paltry motive to live for himself, he found continuing motivation at the deepest levels of consciousness for leading a long, healthy, active, fulfilling life.

✳

When you live for yourself, driven by desires for personal achievement, you cannot help believing that you are the operator, the one who does everything, the one who is at the wheel. As a result you cannot help getting caught in the results of your activities, elated by success and dejected by failure. Even great humanitarians seldom glimpse the magnificent truth the mystics try to show us: the real Operator is not this little, personal 'I' but the Atman, our real Self. Not understanding this, they get consumed by anxiety as to whether their efforts will end in victory or defeat. Gandhi worked tirelessly for the uplift of the Indian people, but by renouncing "the fruits of action" – any personal benefit – he freed himself from the oppressive sense of being the operator or doer.

"You have the right to action," says the Bhagavad Gita, "but not to the results of action." Anxiety about results – fear of not getting our own way, fear of not getting the results which seem to us to be the best – causes depletion and exhaustion. If we can work hard toward a selfless goal using selfless means, giving up every desire for the fruits of action, we shall work at our best in success and defeat. Then even defeat becomes an opportunity.

It is not possible to be detached from the results of action without some deep degree of spiritual experience. The deeper our spiritual awareness, the more we have freed ourselves from the tyranny of self-will which makes us believe that we are the agents of action.

"How do I free myself from the belief that I am the operator? How do I empty myself of self-will in order that 'Thy will be done'? How can I know what is my will and what is Thy will? How can I empty myself of myself and become, in Saint Francis's words, a perfect 'instrument of Thy peace'?" These questions are answered in meditation when we practice it sincerely, systematically, and with sustained enthusiasm. The answers do not come through voices or visions, but through slow, steady growth in discrimination and detachment. As old desires lose their power to drive us, veil after veil falls away from our eyes, leaving our vision calm and clear, able to take in the whole where before we saw only our own small corner.

It is when I see only my own corner of life that I believe I am here and joy is out there. Once I see the whole, in the climax of meditation called *samadhi*, I know I am there as well as here. I am in everyone and everything, and everyone and everything is in me. No more do I need to chase rainbows; no more am I driven by the need to possess people and things. I am complete.

The Secret of Happiness

WHEN I FIRST came to this country, more than thirty years ago, I traveled on a British Peninsular and Oriental liner as far as Marseilles. I had never been outside India before; in fact, I'd never been on a ship. So when I received an invitation to attend the captain's party, I looked forward to it with interest. I thought in my simplicity, "This is the kind of event I have been reading about in literature all these years, where champagne flows like water and wit sparkles like champagne."

Three hundred people showed up that night, and I have never seen a grimmer crowd on land or sea. Everybody was wearing the same look of dark determination: "I'm going to be happy even if it kills me."

This is the spirit in which most of us go about today: I'm going to be happy even if it kills me. Ecologists and physicians are beginning to tell us, "Don't be surprised if it does."

If we look with some detachment on the moments when we were truly happy, we will find that it was not when we were at a party or watching a movie. It was when we were so quietly, completely absorbed in something that we forgot ourselves altogether. That is the secret of happiness. In forgetting about ourselves – our problems, our needs, our quirks and prepossessions – we become happy, just as in dwelling on ourselves we make ourselves miserable.

Down through the ages, mystics from all traditions have been telling us how to get this self-centered little 'I' out of the way to make room for the big 'I,' our real Self, which is the source of joy. Unfortunately, most trends in our civilization are in the opposite direction: "Think about yourself always." What they are really saying is, "Don't ever be happy."

When my niece was with us in California some years ago, she had her heart set on being a hopscotch champion. It seemed to me that she was making good progress, but the subtleties of the game escaped me. So finally I asked her, "What's the secret of championship hopscotch?"

Her answer was right to the point: "Small feet."

Even I could appreciate that. If you have constable's feet, so long and broad that they cut across all the lines, you can't get anywhere in hopscotch. Life is like that too: if you have a big ego, you can't go anywhere without fouling on the lines. But there are people who have petite, size five egos, who find it easy to remember the needs of others. They may not have much money or be highly educated, but they are loved wherever they go.

Sometimes on the freeway I see an immense mobile home being pulled along by a truck. Warning flags stick out all over, and a big red sign at the back warns, "Wide Load." Everybody knows what it means: "Watch out! I'm not going to fit in my own lane, so I'm going to take up some of yours too."

This is what people with big egos are like. They career along on their own personal trips oblivious of the traffic around them, blocking other people, getting their elbows in their neighbors' ribs, and sometimes even causing an accident. For people like this, life can really be miserable. It is difficult to be with them, difficult for them to be with others; they are lonely wherever they go.

Unfortunately, this is the tenor of our times. I was reading not long ago that the number of men and women living alone in this country has doubled in recent years. It is a sobering comment on what inflated self-will can do. When some of these people were interviewed, the reasons they gave for choosing to live by themselves were often worthy of a three-year-old child. "When I come home from work," one said, "I like to throw my clothes wherever I want." She was serious. Another said, "I like to turn up my stereo as loud as I want." And a third: "I don't like to have to argue about what I'm going to watch on television." All this is said in the name of freedom, but I would say these are rigid people, with no freedom in their lives at all. Because they find it impossible to live with others, they end up unable to live even with themselves.

*

To keep the ego from becoming inflated, it is essential to have active personal relationships. Without other people to relate to, we end up brooding more and more on ourselves, until finally we live in a world of one. If we find it difficult to get along with others, that is just the reason to be with them more. Difficulty in relationships is a clear warning signal: "Watch out! The ego-load is getting wider." It is in the give-and-take of life that we learn to be flexible, to smooth out the angles and corners of our personality so that we can relate easily to those around us.

All the great traditions of mysticism agree that to take to the spiritual life, it is not necessary to withdraw from society. We do not have to leave our family and community and retire to Mount Athos, or try to discover the harmony of nature in the jungles of a Micronesian island. For some, of course, the cloister is the right place; this is a matter of individual temperament and choice. But spiritual values can be lived anywhere: with our family, at work, wherever we are.

If you ask the man in the street about Saint Teresa of Avila or Saint Francis of Assisi, you will often get some comment like, "Visionary. Impractical. Couldn't keep their feet on the ground." Because their inner life is so profound, we think they have turned their backs on living. But one of the most practical reasons why the mystics turn their attention inwards in meditation is to tap the power for solving problems that come up throughout the day.

This is very much like getting momentum in a track event. A few years ago, watching the Olympics on television, I was surprised to see how far back some of these athletes went to get a running start. In the pole vault one chap walked up to the bar, then turned around and strode so far back that I thought he had decided to go home. If you didn't know about the pole vault you might think, "What's the matter with this fellow? Instead of competing, he's running away." He's not running away; he's going back to get the momentum he needs for a really big jump.

That is the purpose of meditation too. Instead of getting out of bed and plunging directly into life's maelstrom unprepared, you sit down for a half hour or so in meditation to get a good start. When you go out into the world, you have a good reserve of energy and security on which to draw to be patient instead of angry, sympathetic instead of selfish, and loving instead of resentful.

Nothing in life is more difficult than learning to meditate. Scaling Mount Kanchenjunga, skiing on the Alps, or leaping over the Grand Canyon on a jet-assisted motorcycle is a big challenge, but these are nothing compared to the challenge of trying to master your own mind. When you are beginning, meditation may not seem so hard. But wait until you get into the deeper realms of consciousness! The unconscious mind is like a treacherous jungle, where wild animals like anger and fear roam at will. To bring the light of consciousness into these vast, dark continents and learn to traverse them safely requires enormous endurance and dedication, and the capacity to keep your eyes constantly on your goal. But when you have succeeded in becoming conscious even in the depths of the unconscious, you can exercise wisdom everywhere. Where you once were angry, you can be sympathetic; where you were resentful, you can now love.

✳

The applications of this are urgent and important. Since I first began teaching meditation, I have heard hundreds of young people confess, "I just don't like myself the way I am. I don't want to be hostile; I want to be friendly. I don't want to leave a string of broken relationships behind me; I want to know how to love and to be loved. Do I have to learn to live with my problems as I am?" I say, "No. Through meditation and the allied disciplines, you can learn to change anything about yourself that you don't like. Any attitude can be changed, any habit can be unlearned, any personal liability can be transformed into an asset."

Look at a person who is always hostile. He or she will tell you, "I am hostile." "You're not hostile," I correct them gently. "A part of your mind is hostile. Your mind is not you; it is only an instrument that you use." The problem is a mechanical one, which means that it can be solved.

If this isn't clear, look at how hostility expresses itself. We may think that it is John who makes us hostile. But if John weren't around, we would be hostile toward Terry, Sarah, or anyone else who happened to be nearby. In other words, the hostility is not connected with others at all. We have simply developed what is called in Sanskrit a hostility *samskara*. By repeated thoughts, words, and actions, we have made a kind of neurological groove in our mind through which hostility and resentment flow by the course of least resistance.

All of us have channels like this in our consciousness. For some they may be little grooves; for most there are at least a couple of channels that are more like the Panama Canal. But everybody develops samskaras of some kind in the course of growing up. It reminds me a little of what happens when young people go to college. I used to enjoy the Berkeley campus in September, seeing all those fresh faces from places like Fresno and Merced – apple-cheeked, guileless, impressionable. But soon subtle changes develop in appearance and behavior. First come clothes and manners that the folks back home find a little strange. They have different things to talk about than they had in high school, and their vocabulary is broadened in ways which have nothing to do with the curriculum. Gradually they become absorbed in "doing their own thing": people get in their way more easily, they are more self-willed, and resentment becomes a more and more frequent response. By the time they enter graduate school, the samskara of separateness which began as a little trickle has often been dug into a deep canal. Any occasion is enough to set hostility flowing, and once it starts nothing can impede it. Then hostility has become part of their personality. In fact, that is what personality is – a Venice of samskara-canals, which we have dug and tiled so well that we think they are permanent features.

Fortunately, however, these canals are not at all permanent. In the same way as we dug them – by doing the same thing, thinking the same thought, over and over and over – they can be filled in. It takes a lot of work to fill in a whole canal shovel by shovel, but it can be done – and interestingly enough, when it is full at last, a samskara-canal makes very fertile soil. We can plant roses there, grow a little orchard, even make a desert bloom.

This is the very heart of the spiritual life: transforming all our negative habits. As Saint Teresa of Avila puts it, it means living in the light that knows no night. We are always aware of the unity of life; patience and respect flow not only to those who like us but to those who dislike us too. If someone gets angry, instead of feeling compelled to retaliate, we have the security to see that he or she is only crying out for help – and we have the strength to offer help, even if it means bearing the brunt of that anger for a while. People who can do this are loved and welcomed everywhere. As Jesus puts it, they are truly children of God, bringing peace wherever they go.

This is the greatest challenge life can offer us: to go against our own selfish conditioning to reach our full stature as human beings. This is the appeal of meditation. It is because we don't have any challenge in life that most of us do not grow to our real height. We need a challenge that is worthy of our capacities, and making money, if I may say so, is not much of a challenge. Neither is becoming famous or achieving power, and as for pleasure, challenge is conspicuous by its absence. But becoming rich in personal relationships, learning to return love for hatred, these things are the most difficult achievements on the face of the earth. Only when we see a person who has accomplished such feats do we begin to glimpse the heights a human being can attain. This is our real stature, and no matter what our problems or liabilities, every one of us can attain these heights through the regular, enthusiastic practice of meditation.

The Ticket Inspector

THE ORBIT IN which our minds travel lies well outside the realm of words. It encompasses regions populated by those elusive things we call thoughts, which come and go like the faintest of shadows. Yet though they are often too elusive to hold and identify, thoughts leave indelible traces on our lives. For this reason, getting hold of the mind is a strategic undertaking, fraught with difficulties and startling discoveries but well worth the effort.

Often we can grasp the workings of the mind more easily by drawing a parallel with some more tangible thing. A couple of days ago it struck me that the mind has a great deal in common with a crowded train station. New York has Grand Central Station; in India I am most familiar with Madras Central, well down on the southeastern coast. Madras Central is vast. As soon as you enter the upper deck you see two huge boards, ARRIVALS and DEPARTURES. From that vantage point you can look on as thousands of travelers descend to the terminal floor to board trains for many parts of India and points beyond. The Grand Trunk Express runs to Delhi, the nation's capital, a distance of over a thousand miles. The Calcutta Mail travels the length of India's eastern coast. The Bombay Mail cuts across the heart of the subcontinent; the Rameshwaram Express goes to the southern tip. The Bangalore Mail travels west to Mysore, and the Malabar Express goes to my native state of Kerala on the western coast. And I must not omit the Blue Mountain Express, which travels to Mettupalayam at the foot of the Nilgiris or Blue Mountain, where I later made my home. With all these expresses and many more local trains, called shuttles or passengers, Madras Central is quite a busy junction.

The scene in the mind is very much like this. When you descend below the surface level of consciousness, it is almost as if you see the same two big boards: ARRIVALS and DEPARTURES. On the arriving trains come physical cravings, messages from sense stimuli, annoyances from the environment; every train is full to capacity. At the far end, the departing trains are full of responses. This too is a very busy junction; arrivals and departures are scheduled every moment.

Why is the schedule of arrivals so full? Because we have taken great pains to lay down incoming sense-ways in highly regular routes. Stimulation from food, for instance – regular or meter gauge – arrives every couple of hours; thoughts of sex, mostly broad gauge, arrive on a moment's notice. Quite a number of minor sensations too try to hitch rides on the trains that ply these tracks. And most often they succeed, for the engineers rather enjoy making unscheduled stops.

If this is our situation, there is no reason to blame ourselves. Most of us have become conditioned to heavy sense traffic throughout our present life, and perhaps, according to Hinduism and Buddhism, for thousands and thousands of years. The routes have become fixed. Electronic signals have been installed to speed sensations along, so that as soon as a car is put on the tracks, it goes. Everything is automated; there is no longer any need for an engineer. As soon as our day begins, all the traffic in the direction of what we are pleasantly used to is routed right in, and the rest is conveniently sidetracked. That is why it is so difficult for us to exercise any serious control over our thoughts.

Trains in India offer three classes of service. First class is for the affluent. Second is used primarily by professional people. Third class, for the most part, is occupied by simple village folk. Mahatma Gandhi always traveled third class, even though the government tried to provide him with private carriages, because he wanted to identify himself completely with the masses of Indian people he was serving. When a reporter asked him why he insisted on traveling third class, he replied with his characteristic toothless smile, "Because there is no fourth." Similarly, whenever I talk about railway travel in India, I am talking about travel third class. It is in the third-class car that you really get the sense of fellowship that makes trains so enjoyable. You not only get to see beautiful scenery, you get camaraderie too.

When you purchase a ticket at Madras Central, you go past a little gate to have it punched by an inspector. Then you enter your carriage and take your seat. Third-class carriages are crowded; even the luggage racks are sometimes occupied by human beings. From what I have observed, sleeping in a luggage rack requires a fine sense of balance, and the capacity to wake up at a moment's warning if you catch yourself starting to fall. To add to the merriment, sometimes a wedding party of twenty or thirty will enter the carriage and begin celebrating right there and then. All in all, third class is an animated scene.

Indians are a talkative people. As soon as you sit down, someone is likely to ask, "Where are you from?"

You say, "L.A."

"How many brothers and sisters do you have?"

This may seem a little personal, but you don't want to be unfriendly. "Two brothers and one sister."

"What is your salary?"

Here most foreigners get taken aback. From what they have read in travel columns, they are afraid someone is going to bite their ear or demand half a month's pay. But the questioner is not really prying into personal affairs; this kind of exchange is part of being friendly. "Nobody in Pinole has asked me this question in the entire twenty years I've lived there," you may say to yourself. Maybe few people have cared enough to ask. Besides, if you do not care to reveal that you earn only six hundred dollars a month, you can answer, "Two hundred dollars a day." It does not matter; these are just well-meant attempts to make conversation.

Then, before the train pulls out, vendors come up to the windows. Their cries of "*Chaya, kappi, chaya, kappi*" – "Tea, coffee, tea, coffee" – fill the air. They also bring around a kind of Indian pretzel that is even more pretzely than those I have tried in this country. Tea and these pretzels is a combination few can resist; even if they are not hungry, most people feel tempted to have some. Finally, at long last, the guard gives the signal that the train is about to depart.

In the days when I traveled on Indian trains, it sometimes seemed that more people traveled without tickets than with. This was not only understandable, it made for a very interesting situation. Once the train started to move, all kinds of people began coming in – from the luggage racks, out of the restrooms. Often they managed to occupy seats intended for ticketholders. More and more of them would squeeze onto the benches, with the result that there was not room for everybody to sit. At such times I would quietly get up and stand in a corner. I had an accommodating nature, and I decided that if these people wanted my place, even though I held a ticket, who was I to say no? I didn't really mind standing.

But then one or two of these free travelers would start singing. They seldom had trained voices or a classical repertoire, and when they went around afterwards to ask for contributions, I thought people paid partly for services rendered and partly to get them to stop. Even to my accommodating mind, this was pushing things too far.

Fortunately, the trains employed an interesting figure called the ticket inspector. His job was to go around systematically and check each passenger's ticket. One student does not have a ticket at all; another, also ticketless, tries to elude the inspector's watchful eye and fails. Then it turns out that a third fellow's ticket expired several stations back. So the inspector says, "At the next station, you three leave." It is done politely, gently, with a parting "God bless you," but at the next stop all three are ejected.

We run into much the same situation with our departing thoughts. Goodwill has a ticket. Compassion, forgiveness, love, wisdom, are all qualified travelers with lifetime passes. But ill will, jealousy, impatience, greed, and resentment have no tickets. They should never be allowed on our trains. The only problem is that we do not know what to do about them. A train of thought starts out all in order, with our blessing. But as soon as it gets out of sight of the station, all sorts of odd characters appear on the scene. We can hardly believe some of the things they lead us to say and do. They occupy the most prominent seats and raise such a racket that we sometimes suspect we have no legitimate passengers at all.

Meditation functions much like a ticket inspector, polite but very firm. While Mr. Greed is sitting in the front row taking in the view, our inspector comes and asks for his ticket. If Greed hasn't got a ticket – and it never can – the inspector says pointedly, "We are about to make an unscheduled stop. There is the door, invitingly open." If Mr. Greed does not take the hint, he will give a friendly push "to speed the parting guest."

We can all learn to do this. When negative thoughts come, we can take them to the door in meditation without getting the least bit agitated and tell them firmly, "Please go." This is a tremendous feat, tremendous in its difficulty as well as in its implications. But all great spiritual teachers tell us, "We have learned this; you can learn to do it too."

*

When we face a difficult situation, contemporary psychology tells us that we have two choices: fight or flight. Here I beg to differ. We may not exercise it, we may not even know of it, but we have a third alternative: to put ticketless travelers off the train. Then the ticket inspector can give their seats to thoughts we desire: understanding, patience, equanimity, goodwill. Instead of reacting against others, we can choose how we respond. When someone is hostile, we can listen patiently and answer honestly without going on the attack or the defense.

The Bhagavad Gita calls this precious capacity detachment. The term is widely misunderstood. We do not get detached from others; that is insensitivity. We get detached from ourselves, from our own ego, by gaining control over the thoughts with which we respond to life around us.

If this is essential to spiritual awareness, it is equally essential even for physical health. When you get angry at somebody, for example, your arteries are constricted. This is not a result of getting angry or a characteristic of getting angry; constricted arteries are part of what getting angry means. Therefore your blood pressure rises, and your heart has to work harder; these are part of anger too.

When you are young, of course, after the spasm of anger is over, arteries and heart come back to normal. But when you get angry or hostile many times, as most of us do in today's high-pressure world, the heart suffers. Heart muscles need a continuous supply of blood. They suffer slow starvation when arteries are constricted or blocked up, and critical problems ensue. A good deal of this damage is caused by our not knowing how to stay detached and therefore patient – in other words, by not knowing how to keep ticketless travelers like anger off the trains.

We can be kind, patient, and selfless on a sustained basis only if we cultivate detachment. And just as anger and resentment can damage the arteries in the long run, I would hazard the guess that sustained kindness, patience, and selflessness can protect against and even reverse arterial disease. Two brilliant San Francisco cardiologists, Drs. Friedman and Rosenman, say in so many words that in serious cardiovascular problems, the outcome depends not so much on what the doctor is able to do for the patient as on what the patient is able to do for himself. All of us can do a great deal to improve our health by keeping our mind on an even keel; that is what detachment means.

I would even go so far as to say, on the basis of what I myself have experienced, that we can reverse any negative tendency in our personality by refusing to let negative thoughts have their way. This is a far-reaching statement, for it means that positive thoughts are already on board the train. All we have to do is make sure their places are not usurped. Love, for example, is our nature. In a sense we do not have to make ourselves loving; we have only to remove the thoughts that keep love from taking its proper place. This is why I say detachment gives you the capacity to love everybody. When you can regulate your thoughts, you do not simply react to people; your relationships are of your own choice.

When I was a boy, if a friend got angry with me, my spiritual teacher used to ask, "So what? What reason do you have for getting angry with him? What is the connection?" I heard this from her lips so many times that I began to apply it. Nowadays when somebody confides in me, "He's angry with you!" I say, "So what? Let him be angry; I can forgive." It helps me and him alike. If I can even take a few steps closer to him, our friendship will become that much surer.

Many people, after trying this, come to me later on and exclaim, "I never imagined it was so hard!" Nothing is harder. Whoever tells you that detachment is "as easy as drinking water," as we say in my mother tongue, knows very little about the mind. Nothing is more difficult; nothing calls for greater daring. But once people understand what detachment can do for them, they clamor for the glory of the spiritual life. Then previous exploits look like fireflies on a sunny day.

There is another compelling reason for learning to control thoughts: our thoughts actually shape our lives. We just cannot get rid of them. Every thought we think leaves an indelible impression on our consciousness. That is why none of us can afford not to be vigilant when it comes to the mind. Every thought counts. Each angry thought we think contributes to our becoming the type who may fly into a rage at the slightest provocation – just as each kind thought we think contributes to our becoming the type who can be kind in the face of the fiercest provocation.

Here the expression "train of thought" is apt. Even on the neuro-logical level, I think, a thought may be said to run along a track laid down in the mind, from stimulus to response. Someone gets angry with us and the train steams out of the station, picking up angry thoughts all along the line. When it reaches its destination, everyone piles out and delivers a lot of vituperative words. There is no freedom in this; the train mechanically follows the track of our conditioning. If it went more slowly, we would see that the connections it makes as it speeds along are not fixed or predetermined. We have many unsuspected switches leading to different, kinder responses. But they are frozen from disuse, and we are traveling too fast to see them. If we tried to take these switches while the mind is rushing, we might derail the train. First the mind must be slowed down, which is one of the aims of meditation. Then, gradually, we start urging our thoughts down tracks never taken before – new ways of thinking, speaking, and behaving, which for a while may go against all our previous conditioning.

Going with conditioning is easy. A conditioned train of thought has all the momentum of a freight train rolling downhill; you just put it on the track at the top and it rushes to its lowest level without effort. Going against the conditioning of a strong samskara feels like trying to push the whole train uphill by yourself. But you are not without help. In India, when a train has to climb to hill stations like those on the Blue Mountain where my mother and I lived, six or seven thousand feet high, an additional engine is attached at the rear to push. Meditation and its related disciplines are like this extra engine. While the mind is complaining, "I don't like this! I can't do that!" and the body is registering a varied list of psychosomatic complaints, a powerful engine is being hooked on the back. Slowly it begins to push us up over what we have conditioned ourselves to dislike in a person, until we can see him or her in a detached light. Interestingly enough, the light of detachment is not cold. When all self-interest is removed from our seeing, we look on everyone with love.

Indian trains have various signs put up for the passengers' information. One I used to see in every car announced SEATS FORTY – though usually a student would long since have removed the first *s*. Similarly, each car had a chain with a prominent red sign: TO STOP THE TRAIN, PULL THE CHAIN.

Wherever saints and sages have traveled, they have left us such a chain: the mantram. Every day we can tug on it a little to slow down the pace of our rampaging thoughts. For years this will be a mechanical repetition. But as our dedication to the spiritual life deepens, our use of the mantram will begin to have power behind it, the power of deepening devotion to the Lord. In an emergency, those few words will express all the need for support, strength, and comfort we have.

Isn't there a film called *The Great Train Robbery*? Mystics tell us about the Great Train Stoppery. For many years, to draw on my own experience, I have been repeating the mantram my grandmother gave me with a tenacity that most people cannot imagine. I made use of every possible moment, because I wanted so deeply to bring my thoughts under my control. Gradually I was able to slow down the furious rush of the mind until it would take whatever switches I chose. If it started out toward resentment, I could switch it over to compassion. If it began with fear, I could switch to fearlessness. And finally I experienced for the first time the stopping these sages talk about. I could not believe that such a sweet silence was real. The clack-clack-clacking of the mind came to a halt; the tumult of the vendors and ticketless travelers died away. All that remained was an utter, rejuvenating silence. That is what stilling the mind is all about.

In the countryside near where I live there used to be a flourishing railway, largely for the use of the lumber industry. Now industry is elsewhere, and nothing remains of the railway but a few scattered ties. Similarly, the mantram tears up all the conditioned routes in consciousness, where traffic has been going back and forth automatically. When these tracks are removed, our thoughts are free to travel wherever we choose. Then we can step into the most flammable situation and keep our mind kind, peaceful, and compassionate – all that is required to resolve the crises that threaten our world today.

The House of the Mind

IN THE SPRING, people all over my former state of Kerala celebrate one of our great festivals: Vishu, our New Year. My mother, who lived with me in California for ten years, was very particular about observing these immemorial customs, and my niece Meera now carries them on. So this year again, just as I used to do when I was growing up, I allowed myself to be led before dawn to Meera's little altar with my eyes closed, repeating my mantram.

"Little Lamp," my grandmother used to ask, "would you like to see the Lord?"

"Yes, Granny," I would reply.

"Then open your eyes."

There in front would be a mirror wreathed in flowers, reflecting my own face.

In that atmosphere of intense devotion, when each member of the family sees himself or herself reflected in the mirror, one of the greatest messages in the Hindu tradition is conveyed much more vividly than words can: Behind the face you are looking at is the Lord of Love, who dwells forever in the depths of your consciousness – as Nicholas of Cusa says, "the Face behind all faces."

The impression this makes lingers long after New Year's Day is past. Afterwards, if you get angry or do something foolish, another member of the family – usually one of the women – may ask, "Do you remember whose face you saw on Vishu?" Even the toughest of my cousins used to feel sheepish and admit, "I forgot."

In the fever of our modern civilization, we too have forgotten this eternal truth: that by whatever name we call him, the Lord of Love is always present in the depths of our consciousness. Nothing we do can displease him. And human life has one single purpose: to discover this divine Self through the practice of spiritual disciplines, of which the foremost is meditation.

I describe meditation in many different ways. Because it is an interior process, taking place within the mind, the words we use for outward events do not apply. Just as a nuclear physicist often has to fall back on figures of speech to talk about his field, those who have realized the Lord in their own consciousness fall back on similes and parables and homely illustrations to convey what cannot really be conveyed in words. Here I would like to present meditation as a kind of inner exploration – a search through consciousness for the answer to the deep, driving question, Who am I?

The other day I passed a part of San Francisco graced with old Victorian houses. Some were elegant but sadly neglected. Others were being carefully restored, one or two so thoroughly that I almost expected the gentleman of the house to come out wearing a stiff white collar and spats. But for many owners, I am told, the elaborate attention stops with the outside.

That, I thought to myself, is very much what we are like – those Victorian houses. The outside is generally presentable, and that is all we usually see. We stand in the street, so to speak, and observe, "What a nice house! Look at that gingerbread, those beveled glass doors, the wisteria draping from the porch, the hedge trained to look like a squirrel. Wouldn't it be nice to live there!" When we talk about people on the basis of appearances, we speak the same way. We see them for two minutes at the post office and come home saying, "I met the nicest fellow today – not like some I could mention." It is no real reflection on our eyesight to say that is how the vast majority of us see. This is the human condition: to look only at the exterior, the surface of life.

But as my grandmother used to say, "If you want the real taste of a mango, you have to get close to the pit." The surface may taste sweet, but near the pit a mango can taste so sour that you feel like going back to the fruit stall and saying, "Here's your pit; give me back my money." This is common in personal relationships too. A man and a woman go together to an out-of-the-way restaurant, linger over a candlelight dinner gazing into each other's eyes, and sweep home on a cloud saying, "This is it!" They go to the movie theater, which is a valuable aid to transitory romances, and watch *When Harry Met Sally*. She cries, he passes his handkerchief, and for a while they are united, two hearts beating together as one – Ms. Perfection, Mr. Right.

Then they move in together. After that, every day is a surprise. Both, of course, are too gracious to put in words the way they are beginning to feel. But if we could hear their thoughts, they would be saying, "This isn't like dinner at Giorgio's!" "It wasn't this way watching *When Harry Met Sally*." Little by little, they are getting closer to the pit. And finally they are writing to their friends, "I've met Mr. Wrong!" "I've been living with Ms. Imperfection."

Most of us, in fact, know only the veranda, not only of others but also of ourselves. Actually, none of us is Mr. Right or Mr. Wrong, Ms. Perfection or Ms. Imperfection. We do have angles and corners to our personality, but deep within there is a core of perfection and purity in every one of us. To find that divine core, however, we cannot stay outside. We need to open the door of the Victorian house of the mind and go in.

As soon as we do this we find ourselves in the hall, where we see a number of mailboxes for receiving messages from the external world: letters, postcards, special deliveries, advertisements, bills, the usual solicitations and junk mail addressed personally to "Dear Occupant." This mail system offers deliveries around the clock; the hall is as busy as a post office sorting room.

I have never seen postal sorters in this country, but in India they sit around a long table. As mail is dumped from huge bags onto the table they toss it briskly into the proper slots, like a cardsharp dealing cards. But even in the best postal system mistakes can happen. You go to your mailbox and find a letter addressed to someone in Cincinnati, and you just say, "Well, even the best of sorters can nod." This happens regularly in the mind. It is not that the sorter has been nodding; often there is no sorter. The mail carriers come along, fling out a lot of stuff, and everything goes in.

All of us have an excellent sorter available. Patanjali, the great teacher of meditation from ancient India, calls him *buddhi*, the discriminating intellect, and he is waiting ready to be called. But very few of us give him a regular job. As a result, we don't have any choice in what messages to give attention to and what to toss into the circular file.

96

Once we get inside the mind and see this for ourselves, we get concerned. For our house to be in order we need a good, trained staff; otherwise there will be chaos inside. Calvin Coolidge is said to have been asked, "Mr. President, how many people work for you in the White House?" Mr. Coolidge replied, "Half of 'em." Most of us would have to say simply, "None." The mind's personnel are not working for us. They are working for themselves, as we see the moment we pass the hall.

First we find a big dining room frequented by five ravenous eaters – the senses. If left on their own they can eat continuously, gobbling up junk food, nibbling at television and the news, gorging themselves on the *Midnight Rocky Horror Show*, sampling sensations of every kind. In a word, they are conditioned. Nobody has ever taught them how to do anything except eat.

Their five cousins in the living room, on the other hand, are workaholics. They don't much care what they do; they just have to keep busy. These are what Patanjali would call the five organs of action. Just as we have five senses with which we think we know the world, we have five corresponding organs of action by which we interact with the world: the tongue, standing for the power of speech; the hands and feet, standing for the powers of manipulation and motion; and the organs of procreation and elimination. The living room too is a very busy place. But everybody is doing his own thing. Like the senses, the agents of action are thoroughly untrained. Each has the power to help or to harm, but no capacity for discriminating which is which.

On the far side of the dining room we see a little Dutch door where the senses go to pick up things to eat. "Aha!" we say. "That must be the kitchen." Sure enough, inside we find a very special chef. His name in Sanskrit is Preya, "Mr. Pleasing," and he knows how to make all sorts of imaginative creations out of sense impressions. He only serves what is immediately pleasant; he doesn't much care what the consequences are. And he is extremely skillful. He can take a sensory pizza and toss it around and around in the air, and when the senses start clamoring he takes it from the oven and passes it out through the Dutch door. Even while we sleep, Mr. Preya is cooking away. Just as they advertise on expensive cruises, the kitchen is always open; you can go in any time and eat as many meals as you can survive.

For the vast majority of us, this is all we know of the house: hall, dining room, living room, and kitchen. But there comes a kind of threshold in life when we are no longer satisfied with this. When we reach this stage we become a real Paul Pry, intensely curious. Something tells us there must be more to personality than this. We start poking around, knocking on walls, lifting the rugs, looking for hidden doors. And finally one of the walls gives back a peculiar echo. All our Sherlock Holmes instincts are aroused. We push carefully at each panel with mounting excitement until part of the wall gives way a little, making a narrow opening through which we can peer inside.

It is dark. All we can make out at first is a little sign: "Beware. Keep Out. This Means You!" For this is an entry into the unconscious, not at all a tame place to be. It takes training, skill, and plenty of daring to descend wide awake into the very basement of the mind. But that is just what all the years of meditation and the other disciplines have been preparing us for: to enter with full awareness into realms of consciousness where few have ever ventured, where many claim it is impossible to go at all.

At first we can only feel our way slowly, just as when you enter a movie theater on a bright day for a bargain matinee. The meditation passage is our usher; its words gradually throw flashes of light on the contents of the unconscious mind. There will come a point at which we see clearly in this "luminous dark," as Saint John of the Cross calls it. Then the world within will be as real for us as the world without – not more real, I should make clear, but no less real either. It is a thrilling discovery, because we know then that we are in the realms where personality is really made, where the thoughts and desires that prompt our actions arise.

We go down slowly, step by step. The descent is full of surprises; sometimes it is very much like putting your foot down on a step that isn't there. But finally we reach the basement. The air is charged with electricity, heavy with the pungent smell of ozone, as if we had walked into a powerhouse. We have. The basement is vast, and as far as we can see there are hundreds on hundreds of dynamos, some large, some small, *tut-tut-tut*ing on and off. Power is being generated everywhere; the room seems to throb with it. But there seem to be no connections, no order, no explanation of what all this is for.

We start to trace the wiring back up along the walls, into the rooms above. Sure enough, these are power lines for the house: the living room, the dining room, and especially the kitchen. But every circuit is separate. Then at last we realize what all those dynamos are, hundreds and hundreds of them: our desires.

The Compassionate Buddha goes so far as to connect desires directly with the organs of sense and action. Taste is probably the most familiar; we know its power. But there are visual desires too, of course, many of them: to see the sunset at Waikiki, to see a girl-friend, to probe inside a human cell, or glimpse a galaxy. If you look at photographs of Niagara Falls, you can see great crowds of people who have come from Pinole and Walla Walla, San Antonio and Tallahassee, to lean over the rails and stare down. That is the power that can be generated by the desire to see. It is the same with the desire to hear. In San Francisco I used to see people from all over the country sleeping on the streets in front of the Winterland Theater the night before a concert just to hear the Grateful Dead.

Touch scarcely needs an introduction. Its influence is so powerful that even in the most abstract contexts I read phrases like "the texture of prose" and "massaging data." And today even smell is clamoring for equal rights. One particular perfume I read about you don't just put on; you "enter into it" – which, naturally, costs you a hundred dollars. But we pay, because when it comes to romance, smell can be an invaluable ally.

All of us have sensory desires like these; that is part of being human. And there is nothing wrong with having them – provided we also have the capacity to say yes to beneficial desires and no to those that will harm our health or lower the quality of life for us or others. But there are other desires in the basement too, not so much sensory as egocentric, or self-willed: desires for pleasure, for profit, for prestige, for power. The extent of all these amazes us. We had thought ourselves relatively ordinary individuals, but here we have a basement throbbing with power. We rush back down. "Hey," we call out, "where's the engineer?"

Echo answers, "Where?" Nobody is in charge. The discovery is terrifying: nobody to regulate the workings of the mind. Nobody to make sure that thoughts are positive, that we are protected against destructive habits, that we have an inner shield against fatigue, anxiety, loneliness, depression, illness.

What makes these dynamos start and stop so erratically? We go on tracing wires until we discover a little room. The sign on the door says simply, "Alive." Inside is a kind of computerized library, with millions of memories loaded on whirring disks. This is not dead information. These are live memories; all we have to do is activate one to set off an emotional response.

Haven't you ever been riding on the bus and suddenly found yourself five years back in the past, recalling the time your girlfriend left you after that big quarrel on the beach? Even five years later you feel so upset that you start drafting a strong letter to her in your mind. And she, if she remembers how unkind your words were that day, will not be able to sleep. Memories are charged with emotion; just touch one and you get a shock. And the computer seems to be on random access. Nobody is minding the system. There is no trained memory librarian, just as there is no engineer. All this expensive, powerful equipment is on its own, running up our vital energy bill, wasting staggering amounts of power, and propelling us into situations where we do not want to be. Up from the back of the computer library runs a narrow circular stairway. Someone must come here once in a while! We go up stealthily, almost to the top of the house. There we find a little trapdoor. We push. The door opens into an unsuspected penthouse, luxuriously appointed – Oriental carpeting, Louis XIV furniture, crystal chandeliers. Whoever lives here has certainly been making the best of it.

"Come in!" an unctuous voice says with surprise. A well-preserved man of leisure is lounging against the bar in a bright red jumpsuit. "Who are you? I never get visitors here."

"Never mind," we say shortly. "Who are you?"

"Why, I'm the master of the house. Ego's my name. Won't you sit down?"

"What kind of master are you," we ask, "who doesn't take care of his own house?"

"I *do* take care of it, my dear fellow. I paint the outside once every few years – street side only, of course – keep the cobwebs off the front door, mow the lawn, put out a wreath every Christmas so the neighbors will say I'm a credit to the block. What more could you ask?"

"The outside is all right," we say. "But inside is pandemonium."

Ego shrugs. "This is Freedom House. I respect my renters' rights. After all, don't they pay their way? I'm not going to bite the hands that feed. If Taste wants to eat more than he should, say, let him work it out with Stomach. Why should I play tyrant and tell them what to do? It's a free country, isn't it?"

In the early days we might have been taken in. But after several years of meditation, our discrimination is sound. This fellow is an impostor. We start looking around suspiciously. There is nothing unusual in the closets, nothing under the carpets, nothing in the big Chinese urn by the corner. But suddenly we hear faint sounds like music coming from the other side of the far wall. "Ego!" we exclaim. "Is there somebody else up here?"

"What?" says the Ego. "What do you mean? Nothing, old man, no one at all."

The music is unmistakable. We pound on the wall and it stops, almost apologetically. "Ego," we say accusingly, "you've got somebody cooped up in there!" It brings back unsettling literary memories – "The Cask of Amontillado," *The Man in the Iron Mask*.

"Scarcely 'cooped up,'" Ego admits. "He's free as a bird; comes and goes whenever he likes. All I ask is he not get in my way, or go around irritating me with that still, small voice of his. Confidentially, old man, I don't think his head is on right. He doesn't know who he is – calls himself "the Atman," you know, as if he's some kind of lord or royalty. Don't pay him any attention; he'll spoil your fun."

We don't need to hear another word; our suspicions are confirmed. "Ego," we say, "we've got to go. Got a job to do. But don't worry; we'll be back." We know what we have to do. It will be terribly hard, but we need to get control of the very source of power in ourselves – get into the basement and wire all those dynamos together to harness the full power of our desires.

The rewiring takes years. But all along the way there are benefits. Our senses begin to obey us; our thoughts come under control. When a big desire comes for something harmful, we gain the power to channel it toward a higher goal. Gradually all the personnel in the house become trustworthy, reliable friends, alert and willing to do whatever we think best.

The last stages of this great engineering project require monumental labor. I have a friend who is a blacksmith; when I pass by his shop I see him working like Vulcan amidst clouds of smoke, throwing sparks all over the place and making a terrible lot of noise. That is how the basement of the mind becomes. The tremendous reserves of evolutionary energy called *kundalini* are rising; we can almost see the sparks fly, feel what the English mystic Richard Rolle calls the "merrie heat" rising. And in the end we have only one enormous generator. Every lesser desire merges in the overwhelming desire to realize the Self.

There is such power in this state that the body glows with health; vitality flows untiringly. But we do not yet have peace in our hearts. Every faculty in us yearns day and night for one thing only: to see the Self enthroned as sole master in our house.

And when everything draws him like this, the Self comes. There is no warning, no way of knowing when. But one day – or perhaps, as Jesus says, "like a thief in the night" – when we ascend to the penthouse expecting to see Mr. Ego again, the Self quietly comes to greet us at the door, and we throw our arms about him as if we would never let him go again.

Mr. Ego is still present. We don't want to be rude, but the time has come. "My friend," we announce, "you are about to be relocated."

"My dear fellow," he protests, "you must be joking. Is this the first of April?"

"Ego," we tell him firmly, "it's your turn to be shut up. You don't have to leave – at least, not for the present; if you behave yourself, there are plenty of odd jobs that you can do. But keep yourself scarce. From now on, the Self is master of the house – and he's never going to leave again."

The Internal Witness

I bow to the Lord who is the internal witness,
the pure Self, the highest Self, the Knower,
in whom we find our unity.

— THE THOUSAND NAMES OF THE LORD

IN THE DAYS when I was attending my village school, some of us boys – my cousins and I and a few of our schoolmates – would occasionally rob a nearby mango tree. Of course, we were always absolutely sure that nobody would find out. But I don't think the owner of the tree was quite in the dark either, and once, exasperated, he went to the extent of complaining to the headmaster of our school. The headmaster became terribly angry. He called all the boys in the class together and interrogated us.

"Raman, who robbed that tree?"

"I did, sir."

"Shankaran?"

"I robbed it, sir."

"Krishnan?"

"I did it, sir."

One by one, each boy said he had stolen the mangoes. Our headmaster was quite sure who the real culprits were, but he couldn't get any evidence. Finally, at his wits' end, he told some of the better students, "You boys should at least give a few hints. Why do you all say you did it?"

We said, "We are protecting the honor of the school." He had to agree with us, and so we managed to escape.

When I got home, however, my grandmother was waiting. Word gets about quickly in a village, and the first thing she asked me was, "Little Lamp, did you steal those mangoes?"

I kept quiet.

"Were you in the group?"

I still kept quiet.

"Even if none of you tells anybody else," she said, "there was somebody who saw. Someone inside is watching everything, someone who never misses a thing."

In the depths of consciousness, beneath the surface of our egocentric personality, dwells the Lord, who is our true Self – ever wakeful, eternally alert. This is the implication of the Sanskrit epithet *sakshi*, "the internal witness," one of the most significant and practical of the Thousand Names of Sri Krishna. When we do something selfish, the little voice inside saying, "Shabby, shabby, shabby," is the echo of the voice of the Self within. And when we feel warm inside because we have helped someone, that is the Self making us feel warm.

For the most part, however, we are too absorbed in personal pursuits to heed these internal cues. As a result, we are always at odds with our true Self. This is the cause of all the insecurity in our hearts. Somewhere deep down we know the person we want to be, but we are so conditioned to look for satisfaction outside ourselves that we ignore this Self, who is waiting so patiently to be found.

Discovering this Self is the greatest achievement possible. It brings with it everything else we have been looking for – peace of mind, joy, security, fulfillment. Once we make this discovery, we are no longer separate individuals. Our life becomes a lasting, positive force which does not end when we shed the body at death. Saint Francis of Assisi and Mahatma Gandhi are such forces, as alive today as they were when they walked the earth in Italy or India. We may not aspire to become a Francis or a Gandhi. But all of us can become at least a "mini-force" if we set our hearts and minds to it. The same power which changed the would-be troubadour Francis Bernardone into a saint, the ineffectual lawyer M. K. Gandhi into a *mahatma* or "great soul," can enable us too to grow to our full height.

When I say this, people sometimes object, "You don't know what I'm really like! If you knew how unpleasant I can be, how incorrigible I am, you wouldn't be so optimistic. I've made a lot of mistakes in the past, and I'm likely to keep on making them too, because I don't know how to change. In fact, I don't believe I can change."

This is where we can rely upon the testimony of great spiritual figures down the ages. Again and again they assure us that they too have made mistakes, sometimes worse than the ones we have made ourselves. They too have caused trouble to themselves and to those around them. From their own experience, they know that it is possible for any of us to reverse direction in life completely. By drawing on the power released in meditation, we can gradually remove every blemish of self-centered thought and behavior that hides our real Self from view. Of course, this requires immense effort. But it can be done.

A few days ago I was watching a woodpecker, a creature I hadn't seen since I left India. This chap had a red turban. While I watched he came and alighted on a huge tree. He was quite a small creature, and the trunk of the tree was enormous. I wanted to go up to him and say, "What, make a hole in that huge trunk with your tiny beak? Impossible. Preposterous!" But this little woodpecker was not intimidated by size. He did not throw up his legs in despair; he just alighted on a limb and went about looking for the right spot to begin operations.

It is the same with transforming consciousness; you have to look for the right spot. In some people it is a particular compulsive craving; in some it is jealousy; in some, blind fury. Each person has to look for that spot where urgent work is most needed.

After checking out possible areas, this woodpecker settled down at what looked like a solid, unyielding spot and started pecking away rhythmically. He didn't just give a peck or two and then fly off in search of a worm, not to return for half an hour. He went on pecking systematically, with sustained enthusiasm, until he was done.

That is the kind of work required to transform personality. Unfortunately, the process is far from pleasant. For a long time, all we are doing in meditation is pecking away at what we want to change in ourselves, and there is not much satisfaction in pecking away. At best it is tedious; often it is downright painful. As Meister Eckhart puts it, the pauper has to die before the prince can be born. The problem is that all of us identify ourselves with the pauper – the accumulation of habits and opinions, likes and dislikes, which we have developed over the years. We think this is who we are, and are not prepared to let it die. We say instead, "This is how I am. This is me, for better or for worse." The mystics reply, "That is not you. These are veils hiding your real face. You have mistaken the veils for the face, the layers of conditioning for your real Self."

Our whole job in life is to remove these veils – that is, to overcome all the compulsive aspects of our surface personality. At present most of us are not even aware to what extent our desires are compulsive.

We do not realize how often they push and shove us about without any say on our part. But when we think, "I would like a hot fudge sundae," it would be more accurate to say that the desire is thinking us. Intellectually we may know that a hot fudge sundae means more calories than we need. But the desire has a hold on us, and we say this is what will satisfy us. Not until we have eaten the sundae do we reflect, "That's not what I really wanted. Why did I go and eat it?"

Not that there is anything wrong in eating sundaes. The important point is that we do not have the capacity to choose. For "hot fudge sundae" we can substitute our own favorite pleasures. Some may not be harmful in themselves. But when the inability to choose extends to destructive habits such as smoking, drinking, or taking drugs, we begin to cause suffering to ourselves and to those around us.

One particularly painful compulsion in personal relationships is clutching for security at our partner or friends. This leads to all kinds of trouble. When we grasp at another person, the real tragedy is that we cease to see that person. He or she becomes merely an object for propping ourselves up in our insecurity. This is an open invitation to jealousy and finally a broken relationship. People with this problem go from one relationship to another, always grasping and always missing what they are grasping for. Unfortunately they can't see what the problem is, because they have lost the power to choose.

The major cause of such compulsions is our obsessive identification with the body. That the sun takes its bath in the sea at night, as we say in my mother tongue, is a very small superstition compared to the superstition that we are the body. When we believe we are the body, whenever we have a sensory craving, we feel we have no choice but to satisfy it. If we don't satisfy it – or try to – we feel frustrated and unfulfilled. It never occurs to us that as long as we identify ourselves with our desires, we can never be their masters. To become masters of ourselves, we must be able to choose what we desire and what we think – which means that for many, many years we will have to say no to a lot of negative cravings and thoughts.

One helpful clue when you are trying to resist a harmful desire is to remember that the real source of that desire is not the body but the mind. Often, to give just one example, I see people in ice cream parlors who are in no need of nourishment. The emptiness they feel inside them is not a physical emptiness, but they interpret it physically because they identify themselves with the body. Similarly, when we smoke we are simply punishing the body for the restlessness of the mind. This is why the physical approaches to these problems which we sometimes read about, such as wiring the jaws shut to keep from overeating, can never be of much help in overcoming a destructive habit. A few years ago there was a lot of talk about methadone being used to relieve heroin addiction. This may be helpful in certain aspects of medical treatment, but most authorities now realize that methadone treatment only exchanges one drug problem for another. The fault is not with methadone, but with any approach which treats drug addiction as only a physical problem. There is a physical problem, but the cause must be sought in the mind.

Once we have traced a desire to the mind, we begin to get some detachment from it. The desire loses some of its urgency, and when the pressure of desire is relieved, we begin to see that most of our desires are not very long lasting. It's true that we may have wanted a hot fudge sundae an hour ago, but now what we really want is some baklava. In another sixty minutes our all-encompassing desire will be to take a trip to Greece. So one of the helpful tips I usually give my friends for resisting a desire is simply to put it off. If you want some baklava now, just tell your mind to wait until you have finished reading this article. By that time, the chances are that you will have forgotten about the baklava.

For the more adventurous, however, an even better method for fighting compulsions is to go directly against them. When all we want to do is to lock ourselves up in our room and spend the day with our favorite Russian novel, that is the time to go out and be with people, especially in doing something that will benefit others. This is a sure test of spiritual progress. When the desire comes to do our own thing, to bask in our separate enjoyment, even if it is something harmless, we should be able to pick ourselves up and throw ourselves into self-less work with energy and enthusiasm. When we can do this, we gain detachment from both body and mind, which means we are beginning to identify with our real Self.

Detachment is important in all the little affairs of daily living. It gives us freedom to be relaxed and secure whatever comes our way. How many of us get upset when the coffee is not ready in the morning? How many arrive at work tense because the traffic was a little slower than usual? When we are in a hurry, when we have to have things our way, we are always going to be tied up in knots.

The other day in San Francisco I saw an attractive book on the art of tying knots. It reminded me of a saying from Sri Ramakrishna, the great Bengali saint of the nineteenth century, that the spiritual life is not concerned with *grantha*, books, but *granthi*, knots. We know how difficult it is to sleep when muscles are knotted, or how much pain a stiff neck can cause. Knots in the mind are far, far worse. But they can all be untied through the practice of meditation.

Untying these knots is our main concern in life; but it is a concern most people find all too easy to forget. Often people looking into meditation and the spiritual life get sidetracked onto less-than-urgent issues. One of the Buddha's disciples, Malunkyaputta, had this problem. One day he went to the Buddha with a long list of theological questions: Is the universe infinite and eternal? What is the soul? Is it immortal? The Buddha politely listened to all this and then answered with a story. "Imagine," he said, "a soldier wounded with a poisoned arrow. The surgeon arrives and is about to pull out the arrow when the man says, 'Wait. Before you pull it out, I want to know who shot this arrow. What caste is he? Tall or short? Dark or fair?' If the surgeon answers all these questions before he pulls out the arrow, Malunkyaputta, what will happen?"

"He will die, Blessed One."

"It is exactly the same with your questions, Malunkyaputta. Therefore I do not concern myself with intellectual theories. All I teach is how to put an end to suffering."

Many people who are sincerely making an effort to remold their lives want to reconstruct the past and analyze it: who did what to you when and how, and how much better it would have turned out if they or you had done such-and-such instead. We can get a curious sense of satisfaction from looking over our mistakes and saying, "What a gallery!" Fortunately there is no gallery, because there is no past. Only to the extent that we dwell on the past can we bring it to life – and it can only come to life this way by sucking our vitality out of the present, the only moment that is real.

On this score the Buddha's teaching is utterly practical. For all of us, he points out, the greatest source of suffering is our own selfish desires. It seems harsh, but actually his diagnosis has some very encouraging implications. Because the problem lies within us, we can overcome it. All that is necessary is to teach ourselves not to want what we like but what benefits everyone, including ourselves.

The other day I was listening to a two-year-old boy trying to get his mother to give him something she thought he shouldn't have. All I heard was "I want . . . I want . . ." and then a prolonged cry. It is one thing for a two-year-old to cry when he doesn't get what he wants. But at some point we should grow up, which means learning to go against our likes and dislikes when necessary. This is something we can work at systematically, simply by putting our own preferences last and the welfare of others first. When we are able to do this gracefully, we can be called adults. Until then we are children.

Suppose, for instance, you have been planning to go to a particular movie. When your girlfriend says she would rather go to a lecture on Chinese art, you should be able to change your plans without frustration or resentment. Or suppose you have been looking forward to Mexican food and your husband comes home and announces that he has made reservations at a natural foods restaurant. You should be able to welcome the opportunity to enjoy what he enjoys, and at the same time to loosen your own rigid likes and dislikes. These are little things, but it is in such ways that we begin to untie knots in the mind from inside. Eventually we can free ourselves completely from the compulsive drive to go after what we like and to run away from what we dislike. Then if something benefits us or others, even if we do not like it at first, we can learn to like it. If something we are fond of turns out to be harmful, we can pass it up without a backward glance.

When we reach this state, we see that our true identity does not rest in either body or mind. Sri Ramakrishna, using a striking image from Indian village life, says that the completely detached man or woman is like a dry coconut. If you shake a dry coconut, you can hear the kernel rattling against the shell. That is the Atman, which is unattached to the body or mind. Most of us, however, are like the tender coconut: if you shake it, you don't hear a thing. The kernel, the Atman, is stuck fast to the shell of the body, and what holds it are all our selfish attachments, our petty, personal urges and prejudices. When these are eliminated, we are free.

The spiritual life, the mystics say, is not to be lived in a cave. Wherever we are, we should remember that the Lord is within us and act accordingly. It is not enough to bask in the idea that there is a harmony to all things. We must express this harmony in our lives by working for the welfare of our family and community. If we allow violent talk or behavior in our homes, for example, we are turning our backs on unity – and adding our own small bundle of fuel to the flames of violence that threaten the world. If we move away from others because they have problems or because they are unpleasant, we are turning our backs on unity. To discover the unity of life, we have to remain loyal even when others try to move away from us. It will help us, and it will help them too.

A number of years ago a young man came up after one of my talks to tell me that he had already discovered the unity of life. In the course of congratulating him, I happened to ask if he had informed his parents of this wonderful discovery. He replied, "I'm not on speaking terms with my parents." It was my painful duty to remind him that parents are part of life's unity too. For all of us, an important step on the path to union is to learn to get along with everyone around us, especially the members of our family. Even if we have had trouble in the past, we can renew our relationships by forgiving wrongs done to us – or wrongs we imagine were done to us – and trying to see the conflict through the other person's eyes. If there is no more room for improvement with family or friends, to paraphrase Jesus, we can always find an enemy or two to forgive.

*

When I was in high school, like most teenagers I occasionally had to hear my grandmother tell me things like, "Ramaswami from the corner house doesn't think much of you."

I would answer, "What does it matter what Ramaswami thinks?"

"His sister says you and your cousin are not very polite."

"What does it matter what his sister says?"

"What about yourself?" she would ask. "Don't you want the respect of yourself?"

"Of course, Granny."

"Well, then," she would say, "you have to earn it."

Everybody's respect can be easily gained except your own. The Self is the most taciturn, the most difficult, the most impossible observer to curry favor with, because he doesn't miss a trick. He has seen everything. You can flatter him any number of times; he will turn a deaf ear. You can place tantalizing presents before him; he will turn a blind eye. And even if you have done enough good deeds to impress the whole world, resisted so many temptations that the local weekly prints your picture with a glowing review, the Self will just wait. "Let us see," he will say. "Let us see if after many, many years you don't get tired of all this." That's why there is nothing more exhilarating than getting a little pat on the back from within. At the end of a long, hard day, when nothing has gone your way and you have had to struggle just to keep your composure from disappearing down the drain, you will sometimes feel this pat from within and hear a little whisper saying, "Well done." The security that comes from this cannot be shaken by anything on earth.

Once we have totally forgotten ourselves in seeking the welfare of others, the wall of our separate ego has broken down. When we see someone happy, we are happy. When we see people suffering, we do everything we can to alleviate that suffering. We have no individual sorrow whose burden we must bear alone. This is what is meant by seeing the underlying unity of life. It is not an intellectual abstraction; it is a living experience in which we see the Lord everywhere, in everyone, always.

The Hound of Heaven

Whether you like it or not, whether you know it or not,
secretly nature seeks and hunts and tries to ferret out the
track in which God may be found.

    – MEISTER ECKHART

IN THE SEVENTH century, the Venerable Bede tells us, an Anglo-Saxon king by the name of Edwin was approached by emissaries from Rome to persuade him to embrace the Christian faith. Edwin took counsel with one of his most trusted subjects, and the reply he received will probably be remembered when the rest of Bede's history has been forgotten.

It must have been a winter evening, with the bitter cold of a Northumbrian blizzard blowing outside the stone hall where the king and his court warmed themselves about the fire. "Sir," Edwin's counselor replied, "it has often seemed to me that our lives here on earth are like the passage of a little swallow that darts in from the darkness into the cheerful warmth of our banquet hall here, lingers a moment, and then passes again out of the window into the cold and wintry night. We know nothing of where it comes from or where it goes; we see only the brief moments in which its flight is illumined by the fire's flickering light.

"My life too is like this. I do not know where I have come from, why I am here, or where if anywhere I will be after death. If your new religion can throw some light into this darkness that extends before birth and after death, it seems to me most worthy of being followed."

In all religions, in all countries, thoughtful men and women have been troubled by these questions more than by any other. *For what purpose am I here? Where am I going? What awaits me after death?* Without answers to these questions, life has very little meaning. We may amass a lot of money, but at the hour of death our fortunes will throw no light into that darkness. We may have enjoyed a good deal of pleasure, but even before we get up to leave the banquet hall, pleasure and its memories will tell us apologetically, "Sorry, old man. We can't follow you there."

With death waiting, we would expect everyone's driving desire to be to find answers to these questions come what may. Everything else would naturally take second priority. Yet when I look around, I sometimes think most of us keep so busy all the time simply because we do not want even to hear such questions asked. It is a sure measure of the Lord's love that whether or not we want to think about it, he will find ways to go on asking until finally we do hear. Many of the tragedies and reversals of life are special delivery letters sent straight from the Lord to our door, reminding us that other activities will bring us very little satisfaction until we discover why we are here.

In a poem called "The Hound of Heaven," the English poet Francis Thompson describes the Lord as a bloodhound, on the trail of every one of us. If you have read *The Hound of the Baskervilles*, you will see how vivid the image is:

I fled Him, down the nights and down the days;
I fled Him, down the arches of the years;
I fled Him, down the labyrinthine ways
Of my own mind; and in the midst of tears
I hid from Him, and under running laughter.
. . .
Still with unhurrying chase,
And unperturbed pace,
Deliberate speed, majestic instancy,
Came on the following Feet,
And a Voice above their beat –
"Naught shelters thee, who wilt not shelter Me."

If this sounds fanciful to our scientific ears, let me give an illustration. A friend of mine, Brian, had two great passions before he took to meditation. One was music in any mode or form; the other, a restless desire to set foot on every place on this planet at least once. But the Hound of Heaven was on Brian's trail. He picks up the scent of Brian's music *samskara* and his nose quivers; he knows that Brian is ready to be tracked down. Unfortunately, Brian is not ready to be caught. He doesn't even want to see this Hound. So he ducks into the first pleasure-pub he sees, where Nashville Norm is playing the blues. Brian thinks he is there because he likes country music. Actually what he finds so satisfying is being free from that Hound.

Finally, after Norm has gone through his whole repertoire and the proprietor is turning the chairs upside down on the table tops, Brian peeks out the door, certain that the Hound has given up and gone away. He starts walking down the street, but there is a panting somewhere in the dark behind him. Again he leaps into the nearest night club, which happens to be holding a flamenco festival. "Flamenco!" he says. "Just what I've been looking for!" And for a while, until the fascination of flamenco fades, the Hound is forgotten again. Brian is absorbed in learning new modes and rhythms; perhaps he even meets a dark-eyed lady whose singing is as exotic as her name. That is enough to drown out for a while the insistent call within him.

In other words, the music is really irrelevant. If it is not folk music it will be flamenco; if it is not flamenco it will be fugues. The underlying purpose in all these pursuits is to enable Brian to escape this nagging Hound.

But finally Brian grows tired – tired of pubs, tired of music, tired of running away. He gives up hiding. Then, Thompson says, the Hound has got him. "Naught shelters thee, who wilt not shelter Me": in running away from God, we run away from life. Brian settles down, learns to meditate, and turns all his desires inwards to discover what life is really for.

Without a sublime, central, overriding purpose to bring all life together, pursuits like accumulating money and enjoying pleasure have no meaning, because life itself has no meaning until its purpose is discovered and fulfilled. According to the Hindu scriptures, all creation moves toward this supreme purpose through the vast spiral movement of evolution. Even if it takes millions of years, they assure us, all of us will eventually attain the goal of life. In the language of orthodox religion, all of us will eventually return to God, who is our real home.

Here the mystics pose a persuasive question: Why wait for all those millions of years to pass? Why go through the travail of lifetimes' worth of heartbreak and deprivation if you can somehow avoid it? Why not take evolution into your own hands, and turn inwards to discover the source of meaning and fulfillment right within yourself? The Upanishads give a vivid account of this momentous decision. Our senses, they say, have been made to turn outwards. As long as we rely only on our senses, we can only look the wrong way: out. But at last, the scriptures say, some unknown seeker in ancient times – someone who had seen through the games the external world has to offer – sat down in meditation and turned all his attention inward like a laser. In the radiant light of *samadhi*, the climax of meditation, he saw his real Self enshrined in joy in the very depths of his own consciousness.

Simultaneously, when he opens his eyes, he sees the same Self in all the people he meets. No longer is he a separate fragment of life. All the barriers between him and others are gone; after that experience he lives in everyone, and everyone lives in him. Not only that, he lives for everyone. He finds fulfillment not in what he can get for himself, but in what he contributes to the welfare of all life.

Because our senses are so utterly oriented outward, we may doubt the existence of this Self. I have even heard people claim that mysticism denies the physical world. A good mystic would answer, "We are not belittling Sir Isaac Newton. We don't deny the Pythagorean Theorem. All we are saying is that we have discovered another dimension to life, another realm – changeless, eternal, beyond cause and effect – on which the entire physical universe rests." As Spinoza, the great European philosopher, puts it, "The finite rests on the bosom of the Infinite." In all religions, great mystics will say just what Sri Ramakrishna used to say: "Of course you can see God! He is Reality itself. I see Him right now, right here, in everyone, all the time."

I have been telling people about this Self almost daily for more than thirty years, but occasionally I am still asked, "Are you talking about something outside us?" Compared with this Self – whom we call Krishna or Christ, Allah or Adonai or the Divine Mother – my own body is "outside." Compared with the Self, my own life is not more dear. Yet this Self is one and the same in all.

I can illustrate this with a simile borrowed from Shankara, a great mystic of medieval India – adapted, of course, to suit our own century and place. On a moonlit night in Los Angeles, if you look at all the swimming pools – there must be almost a million of them – you will find a moon in every pool. Just as each of those million pool owners says, "This is *my* swimming pool," he or she will say, "This is *my* moon. I've got a swimming pool with moon." Gradually they all come to believe that it really is their moon – theirs and nobody else's.

Shankara just smiles. "As long as you are looking down," he says, "it *is* your moon – a million separate moons. But if you lift up your eyes you will see there is only one real moon, lovely and flaxen, reflected in all these pools."

We have been looking down at our feet throughout evolution; we have forgotten that it is also possible to look up. We have grown used to hanging our heads. When our spiritual teacher encourages us to look upward, we say, "We can't. We're in the habit of focusing our attention on our toes." Our teacher lovingly tries to lift our chins, gives our necks a gentle massage, and over a period of time through his example he shows us how to lift up our eyes. And finally we learn. "Oh! *There's* the moon! There is only one, shining in a whole sky – the same moon for all of us, reflected in every swimming pool in L.A."

This is the tremendous vision that comes in samadhi. Afterwards we know from direct experience that there is only one Self. When we see Africans we know they are all us, only wearing different-colored jackets. When we see children playing in the park in Peking, we exclaim, "Those are *our* children, only they're giggling in Chinese!" It is impossible to separate even the needs of one country from those of another, our outlook has become so universal. Everywhere we see life whole.

This is not merely the opinion of mystics. Though realizing the unity of life is much more than a merely intellectual discovery, great scientists too have expressed the same idea. Here is Albert Einstein:

> A human being is part of the whole, called by us "universe," a part limited in time and space. He experiences himself, his thoughts and feelings, as something separate from the rest – a kind of optical delusion of consciousness. This delusion is a kind of prison for us, restricting us to our personal desires and to affection for a few persons nearest to us. Our task must be to free ourselves from this prison by widening our circle of compassion to embrace all living creatures and the whole of nature in its beauty.

Where war is concerned, for example, it does not take a mystic to see that this narrow idea of national interest which we cling to so dangerously today – "your welfare is either allied with ours or against ours" – is nothing but an "optical delusion." When we regain our sight we see clearly that every country is ours; all people on earth are our own.

Similarly, all creatures are our kith and kin. One of the reasons I enjoy walking on the beach so much is that I see so many of my fellow creatures at close quarters: pelicans, sea gulls, sandpipers, and a sea lion who has become so used to our visits that he waits near shore just to wave his flipper at us. I see him almost every day. They can be so human! Today I saw two sandpipers having a thoroughly modern confrontation, eyeball to eyeball. One poor fellow became so angry that his feathers all stood up. I could imagine what he would have been shrieking if he were human; it made me glad I do not understand sandpiperese. He was pacing up and down on the sand with such fury that I wanted to give him a mantram; it would have quieted him considerably.

For those who realize their oneness with all creation, each moment is imbued with meaning and purpose. Every morning a mystic like Sri Ramakrishna or Teresa of Avila gets up with a different question than most of the rest of the world. We ask, "How big a check can I bring home today? Which pleasure can I manage to work into my schedule? On whom can I vent my wrath?" The mystic asks simply, "How much can I give today and to how many?" This one question reverses our perspective completely. Such a person may look like everyone else, but inwardly he or she embraces the whole of life.

I sometimes hear that the spiritual life means leaving society behind. By no means! The spiritual life means extending a loving arm to society and helping it to go forward. It means contributing in whatever field we can – as teachers, plumbers, nurses, parents – not to gain attention or a fat bank account, but for the sheer joy of giving.

I must have heard many times the same tired objection: "Yes, yes, we appreciate this motive, but you have to take into account the vagaries of human nature. Without profit and pleasure, there is no motivation." This does great injustice to human nature, for it takes it at its lowest level. Human beings give their highest out of love.

This is the challenge that the mystics of all religions hold up to us. It is a challenge meant for heroes and heroines. When all is said and done, making money is not much of a challenge. Enjoying pleasure requires no special talent. But to take our evolution into our own hands, *that* is a real challenge. We have to learn to do something that the conquerors of the external world usually find impossible: to forget our private needs when necessary, so that we can gradually expand our consciousness until it includes the whole of life.

This is never an easy process. Sometimes it is exasperating, even painful. For a while, we may feel we are losing everything – missing out on personal pleasures, falling short of joy. It takes time to realize that nothing of value has been lost; nothing is taken away. Francis Thompson puts it beautifully at the end of his poem, when the Hound of Heaven says after tracking him down at last:

> All which I took from thee I did but take
> Not for thy harms,
> But that thou might'st seek it in My arms.
> All which thy child's mistake
> Fancies as lost, I have stored for thee at home.

The Path of Meditation

THERE IS NOTHING like meditation on earth. Each day it is new to me and fresh. I find it difficult to understand why everyone does not take to it. Millions dedicate their lives to art, music, literature, or science, which reveal just one facet of the priceless jewel hidden in the world. A life based on meditation on the Lord of Love within penetrates far beyond the multiplicity of existence into the indivisible realm of reality, where dwell infinite truth, joy, and beauty.

In meditation I see a clear, changeless goal far above the fever and fret of the day. This inner vision fills me with unshakable security, inspires me with wisdom beyond the reach of the intellect, and releases within me the capacity to act calmly and compassionately.

Until I took to meditation, I could not even conceive of the existence of this higher dimension. Once I began, I had to search for it through years of apparently unrewarding labor and recurring periods of anguish and agony, doubt and despair. It took many years of systematic, sustained practice to dispel the enveloping fog produced by the restless mind in its frantic search for fulfillment in the world without.

When this fog is dispelled completely, the Shvetashvatara Upanishad tells us what we shall see:

> In the depths of meditation sages
> Saw within themselves the Lord of Love,
> Who dwells in the heart of every creature.
> Deep in the hearts of all he dwells, hidden
> Behind the *gunas* of law, energy,
> And inertia. He is the One; he rules
> Over time, space, and causality.

I am a very ordinary man, who has made the common mistakes most of us commit in our ignorance. But through the blessing of my spiritual teacher, my mother's mother, I was enabled to turn inwards in search of "the Lord of Love, who dwells in the heart of every creature." In my search I followed a systematic program utilizing every aspect of daily living, not withdrawing from family and society but participating in life to the fullest measure possible. My experience fits more or less into the traditional period of *sadhana* or spiritual disciplines referred to by the sages, but even a lifetime is a small offering for so precious a jewel. We do not need to wait until the great culmination of our sadhana to reap rewards. As our attitudes and actions become focused on an overriding goal, integration takes place at the deepest level in character, conduct, and consciousness. Sri Krishna asks in the Bhagavad Gita: "How can you use all your intelligence without being integrated? How can you use all your creative faculties without being integrated? How can you be at peace without being integrated? How can you be happy without being integrated?" Meditation is integration.

On the strength of my own experience, I offer here an eight-point program which can be followed by every person capable of some resolution, some endurance, and some sense of dedication.

1. MEDITATION ON A PASSAGE. Most of us have grasshopper minds, dispersing our attention, energy, and desires in all sorts of directions and depriving us of the power to draw upon our deeper, richer resources for creative living. Using an inspirational passage for meditation every day, as instructed below, helps to slow down the furious, fragmented activity of the mind so that we can gain control over it. The slow, sustained concentration on the passage drives it deep into our minds. Whatever we drive deep into consciousness, that we become. "All that we are," declares the Buddha, "is the result of what we have thought."

* Meditate for half an hour every morning, as early as is convenient. Do not increase this period; if you want to meditate more, have half an hour in the evening also, preferably at the very end of the day.

* Set aside a room in your home to be used only for meditation and spiritual reading. After a while that room will become associated in your mind with meditation, so that simply entering it will have a calming effect. If you cannot spare a room, have a particular corner. But whichever you choose, keep your meditation place clean, well-ventilated, and reasonably austere.

✻ Sit in a straight-backed chair or on the floor and gently close your eyes. If you sit on the floor, you may need to support your back lightly against a wall. You should be comfortable enough to forget your body, but not so comfortable that you become drowsy.

✻ Whatever position you choose, be sure to keep your head, neck, and spinal column erect in a straight line. As concentration deepens, the nervous system relaxes and you may begin to fall asleep. It is important to resist this tendency right from the beginning, by drawing yourself up and away from your back support until the wave of sleep has passed.

✻ Then, in your mind, go *slowly* through an inspirational passage from the scriptures or the great mystics. For example, you might begin with the Prayer of Saint Francis of Assisi:

> Lord, make me an instrument of thy peace.
> Where there is hatred, let me sow love;
> Where there is injury, pardon;
> Where there is doubt, faith;
> Where there is despair, hope;
> Where there is darkness, light;
> Where there is sadness, joy.
>
> O divine Master, grant that I may not so much seek
> To be consoled as to console,
> To be understood as to understand,
> To be loved as to love;
> For it is in giving that we receive,
> It is in pardoning that we are pardoned,
> It is in dying to self that we are born to eternal life.

∗ Do not follow any association of ideas or try to think about the passage. If you are giving your attention to the words, the meaning has to sink in. When distractions come, do not resist them, but try to give more and more attention to the words of the passage. If your mind strays from the passage completely, bring it back gently to the beginning and start again.

∗ When you reach the end of the passage, you may use it again and again until you have memorized others. It is helpful to have a wide variety of passages for meditation, drawn from all the world's major traditions. I recommend chapters two and twelve of the Bhagavad Gita, the Lord's Prayer, the Twenty-third Psalm, the Beatitudes, and the first chapter of the Dhammapada of the Buddha. I have also translated some of the Upanishads for use in meditation. Whatever you choose, the passage should be positive and practical, chosen from a major scripture or a mystic of the highest stature.

The secret of meditation is simple: you become what you meditate on. When you use the Prayer of Saint Francis every day in meditation, you are driving the words deep into your consciousness. Eventually they become an integral part of your personality, which means they will find constant expression in what you do, what you say, and what you think.

2. REPETITION OF A MANTRAM. A mantram is a powerful spiritual formula which, when repeated silently in the mind, has the capacity to transform consciousness. There is nothing magical about this. It is simply a matter of practice, as all of us can verify for ourselves.

Every religious tradition has a mantram, often more than one. The name of Jesus itself is a powerful mantram; Catholics also use *Hail Mary* or *Ave Maria*. Jews may use *Barukh attah Adonai;* Muslims repeat the name of Allah or *Allahu akbar*. Probably the oldest Buddhist mantram is *Om mani padme hum,* referring to the "jewel in the heart." And in Hinduism, among many choices, I recommend *Rama, Rama,* which was Mahatma Gandhi's mantram, or the longer mantram which I received from my own spiritual teacher, my grandmother:

> Haré Rama Haré Rama
> Rama Rama Haré Haré
> Haré Krishna Haré Krishna
> Krishna Krishna Haré Haré

Select a mantram that appeals to you deeply. Then, once you have chosen, do not change your mantram again. Otherwise, as Sri Ramakrishna puts it, you will be like a man digging shallow wells in many places; you will never go deep enough to find water.

Repeat your mantram silently every time you get the chance: while walking, while waiting, while doing mechanical chores like washing dishes, and especially when you are falling asleep. You will find that this is not mindless repetition; the mantram will help to keep you relaxed and alert. Whenever you are angry or afraid, nervous or worried or resentful, repeat the mantram until the agitation subsides. The mantram works to steady the mind, and all these emotions are power running against you which the mantram can harness and put to work.

3. SLOWING DOWN. In the modern world we are conditioned to live faster and faster. We are only beginning to see that speed makes for tension, surface-living, and insecurity.

It is not enough to talk about this; we must learn to slow down the pace of our lives. To do this it is a great help to start the day early; that is how you set the pace for the day. Have your meditation as early as possible. Don't rush through breakfast. Allow enough time to get to work without haste. At any time during the day when you catch yourself hurrying, repeat the mantram to slow down.

In order to slow down, it is necessary gradually to eliminate activities outside your job and family responsibilities which do not add to your spiritual growth. At first people feel at a loss for what to do with the time they save by dropping courses in kite-making and flower arrangement. What we lose in activity we gain in intensity by learning to rest content on each moment. The British poet John Donne says, "Be your own home and therein dwell." We can find our center of gravity within ourselves by simplifying and slowing down our lives.

It is essential in this connection not to confuse slowness with sloth, which breeds procrastination and general inefficiency. In slowing down, attend meticulously to details, giving the very best you are capable of even to the smallest undertaking.

4. ONE-POINTED ATTENTION. People today split their attention in many ways. Background music while we eat, study, or work prevents us from being fully aware of what we are eating, studying, or working at. Smoking while watching a movie curtails our capacity to appreciate the movie. In all these activities the mind is two-pointed. Everything we do should be worthy of our fullest attention. This is making the mind one-pointed, which means utilizing all its resources.

When you are talking with someone, give him your full attention.

Look only at him. Listen only to him, no matter what distractions come in the way. When you give someone your complete attention, that helps him to give his best attention to you. Gradually, over a period of years, this becomes an effortless pattern of graceful behavior.

5. TRAINING THE SENSES. "Stimulate the senses" is the slogan of the mass media around us. One Western historian goes to the extent of calling our modern civilization sensate. Therefore, we have to be extremely vigilant to ensure that we do not come under the tyranny of the senses.

Our five senses are much like puppies. When we let them do as they like, they may end up ruining the whole house. If we train them, they become sensitive, responsive, and free from conditioning. The senses must be obedient if we are to live in freedom. This is not a plea for sense-denial, but for training the senses to be clear and strong. Indulgence blunts the fine edge of the senses, jangles the nervous system, adds to the restlessness of the mind, and clouds the judgment.

In order to train our senses, we have to exercise discriminating restraint over the food we eat, the books we read, the movies we see, the music we listen to, and the places we frequent. Food is an important place to begin. Mahatma Gandhi was fond of pointing out that control of the palate is a valuable aid in controlling the mind. When we misinterpret a sense craving as a hunger signal, we often overload a stomach that is already full. To control such cravings, eat only when hungry and eat temperately. Have a balanced diet, preferably from a variety of whole-food sources, and eat plenty of fresh fruits and vegetables. Avoid strongly flavored, spiced, overcooked, and deep-fried foods.

6. PUTTING OTHERS FIRST. I place a good deal of emphasis on the family, for it provides countless opportunities every day for expanding our consciousness by reducing our self-will, selfishness, and separateness. Dwelling on oneself always constricts consciousness. To the extent that we put the welfare of others first, we break out of the prison of our own separateness.

When we dwell on ourselves, we build a wall between ourselves and others. Those who keep thinking about *their* needs, *their* wants, *their* plans, *their* ideas cannot help being lonely and insecure. The simple but effective technique I suggest is to learn to put other people first within the circle of your family and friends, where there is already a basis of love on which to build. When husband and wife try to put each other first, for example, they are not only moving closer to each other; they are removing the barriers of their ego-prison, which deepens their relationships with everyone else as well.

7. SPIRITUAL FELLOWSHIP, or *satsang*. When trying to change our life, we need the support and companionship of others with a similar goal. If you have friends who are meditating along the lines suggested here, you can get together regularly to share a vegetarian meal, meditate, and perhaps read and discuss inspiring, practical spiritual works. Share your times of entertainment too; relaxation is an important part of spiritual living. Who has ever seen a mystic with a sour face?

8. SPIRITUAL READING. We are so immersed these days in what the mass media offer that it is very helpful to give half an hour or so each day to reading the scriptures and writings of great mystics like Saint Teresa and Sri Ramakrishna who have verified

the scriptures in their lives. We can cultivate a universal outlook by steeping ourselves in the spiritual awareness of the mystics of all religions, countries, and epochs. Just before bedtime, after evening meditation, is a particularly good time for such reading, because the thoughts you fall asleep in will be with you throughout the night.

*

By practicing this eight-point program all our life, we can learn "to love the Lord with all our heart and with all our soul and with all our might." It is then that he reveals himself to us in the depths of our consciousness through an act of infinite grace. "He who approaches near to Me one span, I will approach near to him one cubit; and he who approaches near to Me one cubit, I will approach near to him one fathom; and whoever approaches Me walking, I will come to him running; and he who meets Me with sins equivalent to the whole world, I will greet him with forgiveness equal to it." So says the *Mishkat al-Masabih*. Or as they have been saying down the ages in India, when we take one step towards the Lord, he takes seven steps towards us. But this first step we must take.

Deepening Meditation

PEOPLE OFTEN ASK me for practical suggestions on how to improve their meditation. Some have been meditating for several years, others only for a short while, but most of my suggestions are applicable to all. They are not taken from books. They are distilled from observations I have made over the years from my own experience in meditation.

To begin with, understanding how meditation works can help a good deal in understanding all the little ways in which it can be improved. Meditation is essentially a process of stilling the mind – slowing down the rush of thoughts until it finally comes to rest. For the vast majority of us this is a long, frustrating process. The mind does not like to meditate; it wants to wander. When someone is not doing very well in meditation, consequently, one explanation is simple: his or her mind is elsewhere.

To be accurate, this is not meditation. It is a necessary preparation for meditation, a kind of primary school for the mind. Patanjali calls this stage *pratyahara*: simply trying to get the mind to stay on the school grounds until the last bell rings. That is all we can do at first. The mind has been playing truant for years; when we try to concentrate, it simply is not present. All we can do is stand at the doorstep and whistle, trying to call it back in.

In *dharana*, the high-school stage, we try to keep the mind in the classroom. It is still hyperactive. It can't stay at its desk; it keeps getting up and running around in the middle of the lesson. But at least it is in school; it is gradually quieting down.

The next stage is what we can properly call meditation: in Sanskrit, *dhyana*. The mind is in college; it has learned to study. When we start it out on a single thought – say, the Prayer of Saint Francis of Assisi – it stays on that thought and does not wander. This happens gradually. At first we may only have a minute or two of real meditation, but that minute or two is tremendous. The mind is completely absorbed in the words of the passage; attention flows without a break.

Yesterday I was watching my friend Laurel decant olive oil from a big gallon tin into a flask. The flow was perfect and unbroken; the thin descending thread of oil merged in the oil below without a ripple of disturbance. That is the classical illustration of how meditation should be. "Laurel," I said, "if you could pour your thoughts like that, you would be in dhyana."

When concentration is complete even for a few minutes, the rushing, turbulent process we call the mind has almost come to a healing halt. In those few minutes all kinds of changes take place throughout the body and the mind. The breathing rhythm may fall drastically – say, to two or four times a minute instead of sixteen. Correspondingly, I would say, other biological processes are slowed down, without our even being aware of it. It is such a deeply restful, renewing state that after a taste of it, we will want it again so badly that we will do everything we can during the rest of the day to make our next period of meditation deeper. One minute of this experience is worth hours of running after the mind to serve a truancy notice on it. But we do not get that minute until we have trained the mind to quiet down.

Logically this sounds like a paradox: you can't still the mind without meditation, and you can't meditate unless the mind is still. Thirty years ago, before spiritual conundrums became commonplace, people really used to bristle at this kind of statement. "You can't get a job unless you join the union," they would complain, "and you can't join the union unless you have a job." But once you try it you see that it is possible, and that there is no other way.

One explanation I can give is that there are really two parts of the mind, a higher mind and a lower. We begin by using the higher mind to control the lower – the senses and passions. In the end we are going to throw them both out; the mind has to be completely stilled. But we don't mention this to the higher mind yet. We just say, "I want you to be in charge. This lower mind is completely undisciplined. You have some vestiges of discipline; why don't you teach him how to behave?" This is a responsibility that the higher mind responds to nicely. Then, when the higher mind is a model of decorum and the lower mind is behaving like the higher, we say politely, "Now both of you please leave." The mind has to become completely still if we are to go beyond it into a transcendental mode of knowing.

For the final stage of meditation I have to change the metaphor. The mind can be compared to a kind of Frisbee, always spinning. We are used to paying attention to the spinning part. But in meditation we are learning to concentrate all our attention on the center of the mind, where it happens there is a little hole – a center of emptiness where the mind is still, which the Buddhists call "no-mind." When we are able to look through that hole of emptiness with our attention completely one-pointed, we no longer see the mind. We see instead the silhouette of our real Self, the Lord of Love. This tremendous experience is *samadhi*, the final stage of meditation. More properly it is not a stage at all, but the climax of all spiritual disciplines.

Once the mind is stilled, it becomes as obedient as a well-trained thoroughbred. As the Katha Upanishad puts it, we actually have ten thoroughbreds pulling us along – five senses and five organs of action. The body is the chariot they pull, we are the rider, and the mind is the reins. For the vast majority of us, these powerful creatures are utterly untrained. They pull this way and that, dragging the mind after them, and we consider this utterly normal. It does not usually occur to us that there is a purpose for the mind: to guide these horses, our senses and actions, so that they all pull together as we command. The way to do this is not to go up to each horse with apples and sugar cubes in our pockets and try to win them over one by one. We make friends with the trainer, the discriminating intellect or higher mind. In other words, when we can regulate the mind, we get control over all our senses and actions.

If chariots and horses are too old-fashioned, let me try automobiles. Meditation is a steering wheel. Take the steering wheel off your car sometime and see what happens when you go for a drive. Most of us careen through life just like that, because the mind doesn't have a steering wheel; all it has is a little hub. The steering wheel is carefully stored away in the trunk; we haven't used it since we bought the car. Stilling the mind means affixing the wheel to the hub. Then we can steer through life like an expert race driver, with a mind as responsive as a Ferrari.

So much for the glamour of meditation. Now we can have a few words about the drudgery, which is an unavoidable part of learning. After all, in every skill I know of, the first part is a lot of repetitious practice. Effortless grace comes later.

As far as the actual practice of meditation goes, try to begin at the same fixed time every day. It is very much like dinner. When you have been eating at six-thirty every evening for a year or so, your stomach no longer has to ask if it is time to punch in. When six-thirty approaches, it knows the time has come for action. Similarly, if you have been having morning and evening meditation regularly, even if the mind has been unruly the rest of the day, it knows these are times to quiet down. After a while this becomes a precious habit. Just as at six-ten you begin to feel hungry for lasagna, in the morning you will feel a kind of mental hunger for meditation.

By and large, unless you are a nurse or work the graveyard shift in a factory, it is good to be in your meditation room by six o'clock in the morning. But be sure to leave ample time to have your full meditation and a leisurely breakfast without worrying about the clock. I used to try to get to work a little ahead of time too. All these help to keep the mind from speeding up again as the day goes on. And come to meditation on time even if you haven't slept well. Half an hour of good, concentrated meditation will do much more to make up for a restless night than will an extra thirty minutes of sleep.

In general, it is helpful to move the body as little as possible during meditation. A still body is an aid to stilling the mind. If you do have to shift your position, do so slowly and quietly, as if you were performing those slow-motion exercises from China called Tai Chi Chuan. Much later, when you become so deeply absorbed in meditation that you are not aware of your body, it will take care of these things by itself without any attention from you. When I sit down for meditation now, I allow myself the luxury of telling my body, "You have been a good buddy, so you do what you like. I am going to do what I like." When I return to the physical level of consciousness, I may find that my legs have made themselves more comfortable without my ever being aware of it.

But this is only after many, many years. In the early stages, if you tell your body "Do as you like," it is all too likely to droop obligingly and fall asleep.

This is one reason why it is important right from the outset to get into the habit of keeping the spinal column erect in meditation. Head, neck, and spine should be naturally in a straight line. This does not mean making your body tense. Straining physically makes you acutely aware of the body, which defeats the purpose of meditation. But on the other hand, do not let the body slump; that is inviting sleep to come and carry you away. If you feel yourself growing drowsy, draw yourself up straight and let the wave of sleep pass over you.

You can make it second nature to check these things for an instant or two once or twice during meditation, just to be sure that your body is not playing tricks on you. One easy way to do this is to check your hands. If they are relaxed, your body is also likely to be relaxed to some extent. But aside from this, do not think about the body at all.

Third, people often tell me they have trouble getting their meditation off to a good, concentrated start. What I do is very much in the mainstream of the Hindu tradition, over five thousand years old. I begin by offering all my love to Sri Krishna, the Lord of Love, in my heart. Then I ask the blessings of my teacher. This is traditional, but it has a very practical effect: it focuses your attention and reminds you of the supreme purpose behind your meditation, which otherwise can get fuzzy around the edges.

This way of beginning is a personal choice, which I leave to each person to decide. But everybody can benefit from repeating the mantram a few times in the mind before actually embarking on the meditation passage; it immediately helps to quiet the mind. In traditional language, this too is a way of calling upon the Self within to reveal itself in the depths of our consciousness.

Usually it takes some time to find the right pace for meditation. For most of us the mind has been racing at top speed in overdrive for many years. In meditation we are slowing it down, gradually shifting into a lower and lower gear. But do not space the words so far apart that you go into reverse. That is what happens when your thoughts turn to the past. After a number of years, I can make out very easily when a person is slipping into reverse while meditating, just from the look on his or her face. That person is not meditating. He or she is traveling into the past, which can happen very easily.

When you can make your mind go through the passage at its slowest speed – which means you have really learned to concentrate – there is a living charge in the words. They fall deep into your consciousness and come to life. As you are repeating them, their application to daily living comes right along with their meaning, and with the application is a personal appeal that strengthens the will.

At this time you are not just meditating on words. You are meditating on the vital applications of an eternal truth to daily living. The proof will be that after you finish meditation, these applications will follow you through the day, to help you make wise choices in what to eat, how to work, how to give your best to your job and to those around you. When you see a situation in which the verse applies, you will almost see the words written across the scene. I often remind those who meditate with me that there is no need for formal midterms to evaluate progress. Every situation is an impromptu quiz. With some experience, you can just look at a person – the way she works, the way he walks, the way she speaks, the way he relates to others – to see whether the applications of the meditation passage are still present. If they are, meditation has been very good; that person can give himself or herself an A. If the applications are no longer present, there is still considerable room for improvement.

For a few weeks in the beginning, you may want to look over these suggestions before meditation every day, just to make sure that they are remembered. They are simple, so some are easily forgotten. But they are so important that if they are followed scrupulously, to the letter, you cannot help making steady progress.

✳

Last, let me share with you one of the most helpful pieces of advice I know, gleaned from experience: never allow anything to come in the way of your meditation. Meditation cannot be done by fits and starts. It cannot be left for when we think of it or feel like it or have nothing more pressing to do. With this one simple decision – "I'm going to put meditation first" – we save ourselves from innumerable doubts, difficulties, and indecisions.

I did not learn this in a cave on the Himalayas. I began to meditate in the midst of an intensely active life as a college professor in India, where the demands on a teacher's time are heavy. Physical facilities are limited, class loads are large, and most of the administrative work is done by faculty. And I was not born with wings and a harp. I was a very ordinary person, learning how to train my mind in a world where there were claims on my time from morning until late at night. Even after I went home, when I had stacks of papers to read and yards of red tape to unwind, students used to come by and say, "I wonder if you could give me a little help with this sonnet of Wordsworth's . . ." Into such a schedule I had to fit time for meditation – first in the morning; then, when I discovered how helpful it was, in the evening too.

I made a list of all the ways in which I was spending time. What I discovered was not entirely to my liking: a significant amount was going to certain pleasant, personal literary hang-ups. They harmed no one. They were even related to my work. After all, I was an English professor; it was entirely appropriate for me to enjoy absorbing lectures like "The Boar's Head Tavern in Eighteenth-Century London." But one by one – not, I admit, without some sense of loss – I began to drop these fascinating pursuits, which were neither necessary nor beneficial. My teaching did not suffer. On the contrary, as my meditation deepened, I became more effective. And interestingly enough, I not only found plenty of time this way for morning and evening meditation, I also found more time for work – time for preparing lectures, helping students, and keeping even longer hours on campus.

In other words, there is no conflict at all between meditation and a busy, responsible life. In fact, so much energy is released in meditation that hard, selfless work and plenty of vigorous exercise are essential. Remember Sri Ramakrishna's pun? In Sanskrit *grantha* means book, *granthi* means knot. Meditation, Sri Ramakrishna says, is not a matter of *grantha* but *granthi* – not reading books but untying knots. It is a perfect image. Don't you use phrases like "my stomach is tied up in knots"? As meditation progresses, all kinds of knots are untied throughout the body and mind. The number of them is amazing; most are knots we never knew we had. In fact, a human being can be described as a collection of knots, all of which are untied in samadhi. And just as a dog that has been tied up for a long time takes off like a rocket when he is released, you and I have been knotted up for so long that tremendous energy is released as each knot is undone. All that energy has to be harnessed in vigorous exercise and hard, concentrated, selfless work; otherwise more energy cannot be released. So do not neglect your responsibilities. Do not have your meditation at the expense of your work, any more than you should neglect meditation for the sake of your work.

"Put meditation first" is a principle I have learned to follow without any exception, as I can illustrate with one or two examples. When I first came to this country by ship over thirty years ago, I was given a tiny cabin with three other Fulbright scholars. There was scarcely room enough for one. Naturally my first thought was, "How am I going to meditate in here?" One of my friends suggested, "Why not take a vacation from it? You can pick up again when you get to New York."

One month without meditation! It sounded horrible. "That is just it," I replied. "I do want a vacation. That's why I have to meditate. With meditation I'm always on vacation."

Ocean-going vessels, as you know, are not designed to serve as ashrams. There seemed to be people in every corridor and deck chair, so that it was impossible to tell which place on board might be quiet and secluded in the morning. It was getting dark, and I was tired. I decided to give my stomach a rest, skip dinner, and go to bed. In the morning I could get up early and go looking for a place to meditate.

I had a top bunk in that cabin – six feet long, two feet wide, the ceiling about two feet from my nose. The associations were a little grim. Since there were also no windows, I decided I might as well have been sealed into a tomb. After a while I got up and found the purser. "I have a problem," I began.

"I can see that," he said. "Everybody else is asleep."

"I need a lot of fresh air at night," I explained. "I would like your advice about where to get it."

"That's very simple," the purser said. "At the head of your bed you will find a little tube. If you open it and turn it where you want it to blow, it will bring you fresh sea air."

I took him seriously. "We can get fresh air!" I told the other fellows in my cabin. "Look at these little tubes." They laughed; they were not interested in fresh air. So I lay down and tried it. That tube delivered air to a circular area about one inch in radius, enough to cool my cheek.

Just as I was determined to get my meditation, I was determined to get fresh air. It was not simply a matter of comfort but of my sadhana. I took my bedding and crept out on deck, where I slept soundly until early morning when a sailor came along with a pail of soapy water and hinted broadly that it was time to be getting up. After some looking, I found the perfect place for spiritual disciplines: the sports deck. Nobody wanted to play volleyball at five in the morning. I sat down with a sigh of relief, and while the salt breeze blew around me, I had my full two and a half hours of meditation.

When I opened my eyes, a group of young Australian men and women were standing not far away, talking about what I must be up to. They had probably been at it for some time, but I hadn't noticed. I did not mind. When you know what meditation can do for you, it will not bother you if the whole world laughs. Whatever the obstacles, I wanted to keep on making progress in meditation.

That desire is the key. I want to repeat that I started meditation just like everybody else. But because of my love for my spiritual teacher, I must have absorbed from her a deep desire for Self-realization. From that desire came a fierce determination not to let anything come in the way of my sadhana. Even though it was painful for me, just as it is for everyone else, I tried consistently to turn my back on every self-centered desire as it came up, because I wanted one thing in life and one thing only: samadhi. In the end, it is the longing for this supreme state – the deep longing which turns your attention away from every passing, personal satisfaction – that is responsible for the mind becoming stilled.

The Candle of the Lord

For Thou wilt light my candle:
the Lord my God will enlighten my darkness.

– PSALM 18:28

WHEN I FIRST came to the United States, a friend took me to visit the Truman Museum in Independence, Missouri. Among the exhibits I saw there, nothing impressed me more deeply than a little clay lamp presented to President Truman by the Jewish community of Boston. This lamp is said to date from the days of King David of the Old Testament. At its base is an inscription from Proverbs 20:27: "The spirit of man is the candle of the Lord."

How this candle is to be lit has been revealed countless times in the history of mankind: by Christ, Sri Krishna, and the nameless seers of the Upanishads, by the Buddha and Mohammed, by Zoroaster and Moses. The principles that underlie all major religions may be stated very simply:

(1) All life, the entire phenomenal world, has as its basis something completely divine.

(2) It is possible for everyone to know this divine ground of all existence.

(3) Life has only one purpose: not to make money, nor to enjoy pleasure, nor to achieve success, nor to attain fame, but to know and be united with this divine ground, which we call God.

I have very little interest in theology, metaphysics, or even philosophy. I am an ordinary, down-to-earth man who looks upon the scriptures as self-help handbooks – practical manuals for the art of living. The truths in them can be verified by anyone prepared to undergo certain universal disciplines, the purpose of which is to still the mind so that it can reveal, like the still waters of a crystal lake, the divinity at its uttermost depths.

"Be still," says the Lord, "and know that I am God." To know God, the divine ground of our existence, we have to go far beyond the senses, the intellect, and the mind. These are but finite instruments, and logic tells us that a finite instrument cannot be used for fathoming the infinite. We require a transcendental mode of knowing, to which the precious experiences of mystics all over the world bear witness. "The natural senses cannot possess God or unite thee to Him," explains William Law:

> nay, thy inward faculties of understanding, will, and memory can only reach after God, but cannot be the place of his habitation in thee. But there is a root or depth of thee from whence all these faculties come forth, as lines from a center, or

as branches from the body of the tree. This depth is the unity, the eternity – I had almost said the infinity – of thy soul; for it is so infinite that nothing can satisfy it or give it rest but the infinity of God.

Lord Krishna, who represents the Self in everyone, tells us in the Gita how we can become aware of this divine center in the depths of consciousness. He tells Arjuna, the prince and devotee who represents you and me, "Still your mind in me; concentrate your mind completely on me. Then you shall be united with me" – not in some afterlife, but here and now. This is the climax of meditation. But Arjuna objects, as I have heard everyone object who undertakes this awesome discipline: "How can I still my mind? It's easier to still the wind!"

"I know it's difficult," Sri Krishna answers. "But there is a simple secret: regular, systematic, steadfast practice."

We have a tremendous ally in this arduous endeavor: the mantram, or holy name. Years ago, when I was living on the Blue Mountain, I taught a small group of village boys how to meditate. Most of them had no education, but I still take pride in recalling how easily they took to this most difficult of all skills. Just like Arjuna, they confided in me how restless their minds were. I told them a simple story. "Last year," I explained, "we had a lot of mice running all over our house. Nothing we could think of could keep them out – until finally we asked one of our cowherd boys to bring a cat. As soon as the cat came in, the mice went out.

"The mantram," I explained, "is like that cat. Repeat it over and over in your mind with increasing concentration, and the three fat mice that keep the mind stirred up – lust, anger, and fear – will leave without a doubt."

*

Meditation develops the most precious capacity that man can have: the capacity to turn anger into compassion, fear into fearlessness, and hatred into love. I am never tired of repeating that this is the greatest miracle of meditation – not seeing visions, nor hearing divine voices, but the capacity to purify the heart, removing all that is selfish and degrading. "Blessed are the pure in heart," Jesus says, "for they shall see God."

Knowing is a function of being. When the mind has become pure, we come to know God because in his infinite grace he allows us to merge in him by what a great Catholic mystic calls "actual participation." The Katha Upanishad describes this state:

> As pure water poured into pure water
> Becomes the very same, so does the Self
> Of the illumined man or woman
> Verily become one with the Godhead.

This experience is the stupendous climax of meditation, called in Sanskrit *samadhi*, from *sam* "with" and *adhi* "Lord" – literally, union with God. Attainment of this supreme state is the goal of life. Hindus call it *moksha*, Buddhists *nirvana*; Jewish and Christian mystics speak of entering the kingdom of heaven within. It is all the same, just as water is the same whether we call it *pani, agua*, or *Wasser*. Those who attain this state of union with God have simply discovered who they are. After that, they have only one purpose in life: to help others discover who they are, by showing them how to realize for themselves the Lord of Love who dwells as the innermost Self in the hearts of all.

The Gita gives a perfect picture of the man or woman who has become one with God. Sri Krishna says, "No one is so dear to me as those who feel the same love for everyone, friend and foe alike. Whether you attack them, vilify them, even torture them, they respond only with kindness and compassion." Jesus tells us the same: "But I say unto you, Love your enemies. Bless them that curse you, do good to them that hate you, and pray for them that despitefully use you and persecute you."

All of us need happiness in life, but all of us need sorrow too. Sorrow can enable us to grow spiritually, and I doubt if there has been any mystic whose heart has not been broken many times before he attained union with God. Therefore, when sorrow is necessary for spiritual growth, the man or woman of God will welcome it with open arms. Put them amidst poverty, amidst wealth; make them healthy, make them sick; make them famous, make them infamous or unknown; they will be the same, because they have identified themselves with that which does not change. Why should they be affected by changes outside when they know the Lord dwells in the depths of their consciousness?

Every moment in life we have this choice to make: Shall I identify myself with my Atman, my soul, with the Christ within, the Krishna enthroned in my heart; or shall I identify myself with the body, subject to change and death? Whether we are aware of it or not, we cannot avoid making this choice; it presents itself to us always. Therefore, we cannot afford to lose our vigilance; we must be constantly, ceaselessly striving. Our will must become so resolute that we will not allow anything to make us swerve from the goal. This is our highest destiny, toward which all mankind moves. Poets, musicians, painters, or sculptors may be artistic, but only a small segment of their personality reveals beauty. The man or woman of God is aflame with beauty; not just one narrow sector but every cell of their being is filled with glory and effulgence.

*

When Dr. Robert Oppenheimer, the distinguished American atomic scientist, witnessed the experimental explosion of the first atomic bomb on the desert of New Mexico, what flashed into his mind was a terrible line from the Gita: "I am become Death, the shatterer of worlds." The devastating word used here in Sanskrit is *kala*, which means more than merely death. *Kala* is also time; and the same line can be translated: "I am time, the destroyer of all, come to consume the world." Time is death. Meister Eckhart explains,

> Time is what keeps the light from reaching us. There is no greater obstacle to God than time: and not only time but temporalities, not only temporal things but temporal affections, not only temporal affections but the very taint and smell of time.

When we practice meditation, we are being delivered out of time, which means we are being delivered out of the jaws of death. In one of the deeply moving devotional hymns of Shankara we are told, "Don't ever be proud of your youth, your wealth, your fame; time will steal this from you in the twinkling of an eye. Take shelter at the feet of the Lord, who is beyond time, change, and death."

In the Upanishads there is a heartbreaking cry that has been echoing down through the ages:

> From the unreal lead me to the Real.
> From darkness lead me to light.
> From death lead me to immortality.

The Buddha was a child of the Upanishads. When, as a young prince, he first saw the afflictions that await us all – disease, decrepitude, and death – the question that burst from his heart was an echo of this prayer: *Is there no way to escape this tragic conditioning? Is there no way to go beyond death?* Young prince Siddhartha gave up his kingdom and went forth into the forest in search of the Eternal. When he returned some seven years later, as the Compassionate Buddha, he gave us the same answer given by Christ in the Sermon on the Mount, by Krishna in the Bhagavad Gita, by the seers of the Upanishads.

Why is it that we see death all around us and never ask ourselves this question: Is there no way to escape death? Nothing else in life is more important. The whole of the Katha Upanishad, one of the most profound mystical documents I know of from any literature, is built around this theme. A teenage boy in ancient India, Nachiketa, goes for an answer to Yama, the King of Death himself. And Yama, after testing him to see if he is worthy, declares this greatest of secrets to have come down through all religions: "As long as you identify yourself with the body, which is subject to change, so long will you be subject to the last great change called death. If you can break through this identification with the body and learn to identify yourself instead with the changeless Self, the Lord within your heart, you will transcend death here and now."

"Teach me," Nachiketa begs. "How can this be done?"

The King of Death replies: "Bring your mind under complete control through one-pointed meditation on the Lord. Anyone who attains this level of consciousness becomes united with God through his infinite grace, and is freed from the cycle of birth and death."

Death is a tremendous change in which the chemical constituents of the body are resolved into another state. You are subject to death only when you identify yourself with your body. Through meditation on the Lord, the Gita says, by identifying yourself with the Self, you can break once and for all this primal compulsion, this age-old, race-old fallacy, that you are the body. As Jesus says to Martha, "I am the resurrection and the life. He that believeth in Me, though he were dead, yet shall he live." Sri Krishna says in the Gita: "Learn to focus all your consciousness on Me. Then I shall rescue you from the cycle of separate birth and death, and raise you into eternal life in Me."

*

"Except ye be born again," Jesus says, "ye cannot enter the kingdom of heaven." One of the most beautiful symbols for Self-realization is the birth of a divine child. Angelus Silesius exclaims:

> Ah! would the heart but be a manger for the birth,
> God would become once more a little child of earth.
> Immeasurable is the Highest! Who but knows it?
> And yet a human heart can perfectly enclose it.

What it means for the Lord, or Christ, to be born in our consciousness is simply that he who is the indivisible unity pervading all life arises in every heart when self-will dies. When the thirst for personal profit and pleasure is quenched once and for all – when the ego is dissolved – there takes place the birth of the Lord.

The meaning of divine incarnation can be interpreted on several different levels. First is the *avatar* – Sri Krishna, Jesus the Christ, the Compassionate Buddha – who comes to rescue the world from the morass of selfishness and violence it sinks into periodically. In the Bhagavad Gita, Sri Krishna promises that whenever violence increases, then in answer to the piteous cry of humanity the Lord manifests himself on earth – as Jesus on the shores of Lake Galilee, as Sri Krishna in the village of Vrindavan, as the blessed Buddha on the slopes of the Himalayas.

But there is another level on which this incarnation of the Lord can take place. One example is Mahatma Gandhi, an ineffectual lawyer in his early life who was able, through the grace of the Lord, to make himself as mighty as the Himalayas. Gandhiji has changed the course of human evolution by showing us through his life that we have really no other alternative than universal love, no other path to survival than to live in goodwill and friendship with all.

Someone once asked Gandhi if nonviolence was the best way to resolve conflicts. "No," he replied. "It is the only way." Love is not a luxury; it is a dire necessity. "Hate and perish, love and prosper" is the choice before us in this crisis of contemporary civilization. By reducing himself to zero, to use his phrase, Gandhi became a candle of the Lord, lighting for our times the way out of violence and self-destruction.

Men and women like Mahatma Gandhi achieve great victories for the human spirit over selfishness, self-will, and violence. But a Gandhi is born only once in many centuries. The rest of us, ordinary men and women who live on what I call the blessed anonymous level of life, each have a critical choice. We can prepare for the birth of the Lord in our own consciousness by trying to abolish every vestige of selfishness and separateness from our lives and hearts; or we can choose to run after personal profit, possessions, and pleasure, handicapping humanity to the extent it is in our power.

In one of his inimitable images, Sri Ramakrishna says that a great incarnation is like a mighty ship that takes people across the sea. Jesus the Christ, the Buddha, and Sri Krishna can be compared to the *Queen Elizabeth*, able to cross the sea of life to what the Buddha calls the "other shore," beyond change and death. But little people like you or me can at least serve as catamarans. *Catamaran* is a Tamil word that has passed into English: *kattu* means to tie, *mara* means wooden planks. We don't have the spiritual capital to build a big ocean liner, but we can improvise by picking up a few planks, maybe a piece of driftwood or two, and tying it all together well enough to float on the sea. That way we may at least be able to carry across our families and friends. Nobody has an excuse to say he or she lacks the wherewithal to cross the sea of life; we can always go on a catamaran.

Sri Krishna says in the Bhagavad Gita:

> Those who know me as their own divine Self,
> The divine Operator within them,
> Break through the belief they are the body
> And will not be born separate again.
> Such a one is united with me.
>
> Delivered from selfish attachment, fear,
> And anger, filled with me, surrendering
> Themselves to me, purified in the fire
> Of my being, many have reached the state
> Of unity in me.
>
> As they approach me, so I receive them.
> All paths lead to me, O Arjuna.

Climbing the Blue Mountain

WHEN I WAS a professor of English in Central India, I used to count the days at the end of the school year before summer vacation began. The temperature often climbs to over one hundred at this time of year, and along with the heat a dry, oppressive wind blows through the streets. Everyone finds it difficult to work under such conditions. In my class I would try every trick I knew to hold the attention of freshmen and sophomores on the exuberant eulogies of English literature:

> Shall I compare thee to a summer's day?
> Thou art more lovely and more temperate:
> Rough winds do shake the darling buds of May,
> And summer's lease hath all too short a date. . . .

But by May our darling buds are blighted, and everyone in India is wishing that summer's lease had never been renewed.

My luggage was ready days before the finals. On the last day I went to campus dressed for the train, and the moment all the papers were in, I stepped into a waiting carriage with bags in hand. By sunset the same evening I would be traveling south on the Grand Trunk Express, going home at last.

India is a vast country. From the Himalayas and the beautiful alpine valleys of Kashmir to the hot, dry plains of Central India is almost a thousand miles. I had nearly as far to go to reach my beloved Blue Mountains, seven to eight thousand feet above sea level, where summer means not sweltering heat but months as mild as any that delighted Shakespeare and Shelley. Even the Grand Trunk Express takes a day and night to travel such a distance. But by the next evening I would be in Madras, far down on India's eastern coast, with just enough time for a cold bath and a good South Indian meal before catching the Blue Mountain Express.

The trip to Coimbatore, across the southern part of India, is hot and dusty. At every stop along the way I would buy tender coconuts, whose milk soothes a parched throat better than any other drink I know. Night brings some relief; but in the crowded cars and sultry air it is difficult to sleep until the breeze begins to blow, announcing the dawn, personified as the goddess Usha, that calls all spiritual aspirants to begin their meditation.

I finish meditation as the Express steams into Coimbatore station. As I open my eyes I see the Blue Mountain beckoning, fifty miles to the north. Here the railway journey ends for me, and the real ascent of the Blue Mountain begins.

✳

For thousands of years, mystics of all religions have used the image of ascending a mountain to describe the adventure of attaining the highest state of consciousness. In Hinduism the lofty Himalayas, which float above the plains of north India wrapped in silence and perpetual snow, have always symbolized the purest realms of spirit. These are the home of Shiva, "Lord of the Mountains," the eternal, perfect yogi, and of his partner, Parvati, the Divine Mother. In the West, among many others, the great Spanish mystic John of the Cross uses the same image in his *Ascent of Mount Carmel.*

These are lofty metaphors, chosen by towering figures in world mysticism. On a much smaller scale, for those of us who are not cut to the same measure, I would like to illustrate the states of meditation with the little journey I used to make every year from the plains of Coimbatore to the summit of the Blue Mountain where my mother and I made our home.

For years the first stage of the interior journey is dull and dreary, like the road that covers the twenty-odd miles from Coimbatore to the town of Mettupalayam. We are not traveling by train now. The rest of the journey has to be made by the kind of rural bus that I still see sometimes in this country, carrying children to school.

The road is slow and teems with travelers. The plains in this part of India have been settled for thousands of years, and from dawn till dusk the road to Mettupalayam is swollen with pedestrians, buses, cars, trucks, wagons, bicycles, and the slow, steady bullock carts that set the pace of traffic. All along the road, just as around a medieval European city, merchants have set up flimsy shacks from which they sell their wares: tea, cloth, grain, vegetables, and the black, pungent local cigarettes called *beedis*. Ancient tamarind trees flank the road; their small, densely packed leaves, green even in the hottest weather, provide precious shade from the scorching rays of the tropical sun. From the window of our old bus the road seems like a ceaseless river of travelers, flowing quietly to and from Coimbatore with scarcely an eddy to break its flow. Most of these men and women have only a few miles to go. When the sun sets, they will have returned to the little place they left. Our destination is much farther and much higher; yet at the end of the day, we too shall have reached home.

The bus reaches Mettupalayam, at the foot of the Blue Mountain. While the driver and conductor have their breakfast, I walk about in the crowded bazaar. Vendors sitting on the pavement call their wares: "Chili-hot *vadai*! Sweet *halva*! *Beedis* to smoke! Hot tea to drink!" I turn a deaf ear and return quickly to the bus. Who wouldn't find it pleasant to linger in the bazaar for the rest of the morning, sampling all the wares? But the bus is leaving, and as Robert Frost says,

> I have promises to keep,
> And miles to go before I sleep,
> And miles to go before I sleep.

During the early stages of the ascent, every spiritual aspirant has to keep saying no when the senses clamor for things that will only add to the burden of the journey later on. "Don't eat this. Don't drink that. Don't smoke this. Don't sniff that." This is all you hear from your spiritual teacher. There is no rapture; there is no ecstasy; only "keep plugging along."

This kind of discriminating restraint of the senses is not asceticism. Its purpose is not to punish or subjugate the body. We need to train the senses to be faithful allies in our ascent, for two compelling reasons. First, the body is our vehicle; we need to keep it healthy, strong, and resilient so that it can carry us steadily and safely to the summit of consciousness. Second, training the senses strengthens the will day by day, enabling us gradually to gain control over the fierce passions that rage beneath the surface of consciousness in every one of us. Without an unbreakable will it is not possible to move up from the Valley of the Shadow of Death; the will itself will turn against us and hold us down. "The will is your only enemy," the Gita tells us, "and the will is your only friend." The will can become our most powerful ally; but left untrained, the will becomes self-will, our worst enemy on earth.

I breathe a sigh of relief as the bus leaves behind the din and dust of the town and crosses the Bhavani River, named after the Divine Mother. Soon we are in the foothills. I glance back through the window. Without being aware of it we have climbed imperceptibly from the plains to the "elevated camp" which *Mettupalayam* signifies in Tamil. That is how *sadhana* proceeds these first few years. From day to day you seem to make no progress. But when you glance back to the year before, though you have a vast distance yet to travel, you realize that you have risen significantly above the physical level of awareness. Your nervous system is more resilient, your will stronger, your senses more responsive, your mind and relationships more secure; your goal is that much clearer before your eyes.

We are above the foothills now. For miles the road winds through a dense forest, abounding with wild animals: elephants, tigers, leopards, bison, bears, and cobras. These creatures cannot be seen from the outskirts of the forest, which entice us with slender, graceful bamboos and colorful wildflowers. But anyone attracted into the depths of the forest will soon hear the roar of a powerful tiger, pouncing on a deer as it leaps for life. These are the dark realms of the unconscious. When we break through the surface layers of awareness in meditation, we come face to face with these untamed passions: anger, fear, lust, self-will. They have always been there prowling, but while we stay on the outskirts of consciousness we scarcely glimpse their number or their power. We do not hear the tiger roaring or the moan of the deer beneath its paw. But that does not allow us to escape the ravaging effects of these destructive passions, which can destroy our health, rend relationships asunder, and bleed us of vitality, wisdom, and love.

These deep, destructive forces or *samskaras* are the causes of all personal problems. Fortunately we cannot come face to face with them until we develop the detachment, dexterity, and determination to overcome them. This is one of meditation's greatest safeguards. By contrast, potent psychoactive drugs can throw you into the tiger's lair before you have the strength and skill to ride a tiger and tame it.

But these fierce creatures *can* be tamed. If you have been meditating sincerely and systematically with sustained enthusiasm, repeating the mantram as often as possible, I can assure you that the mantram will come to your rescue in every one of these jungle encounters. When you can repeat it deep in the unconscious, the mantram releases immense inner resources. You will have to struggle for many years, but in the end every selfish passion can be overcome: not repressed, not destroyed, but brought over to your service and trained. Then the power of fear is transformed into fearlessness, anger into compassion, hatred and resentment into love.

✳

Now we are three thousand feet above sea level. Spread out below is the fertile district of Coimbatore, with the Bhavani River, like the Divine Mother herself, nourishing the fields, trees, animals, villages, and cities of the land. *The Hymn to the Divine Mother as Bhavani,* composed more than a thousand years ago by the great Kerala mystic Shankara, wells up in my heart:

> In times of war or strife or sorrow,
> Of danger whether at home or abroad,
> From flood and fire, in forest or mountains,
> Or amidst my enemies, Mother, protect me!
> You are my source, my path, my goal;
> You alone are my refuge, Bhavani.

The mountain slopes grow steeper. We pass a school team practicing rock climbing; a single rope binds them in safety to one another and to their teacher. By this stage in sadhana, we know first-hand that the meditation passage is our lifeline at these heights of consciousness. One end is fastened securely to our teacher, who has traveled this way before. He knows just where to tell us to put our feet and drive in pitons, where to belay, what false steps to avoid. Even a sincere aspirant may glance down and panic, or miss a foothold, and slip or even fall. But as long as we hold fast to our teacher, practicing all the disciplines of sadhana precisely as instructed, we will always be safe.

It is marvelous to watch this team of dedicated, aspiring young climbers on these precipitous slopes, each tied to the one ahead and all tied together to their teacher. Life is like that, a vast web of delicate relationships binding us together in love. As Francis Thompson says,

> All things by immortal power
> Near or far,
> Hiddenly
> To each other linked are,
> That thou canst not stir a flower
> Without troubling of a star. . . .

If we destroy those ties of unity, we fall. If we care for and preserve them, even if it means ignoring our own personal pleasures and profit, we thrive. As Sri Krishna says in the Gita, this is seeing the Lord in everyone, everywhere, every minute.

By now the hot air of the tropical plains lies far behind us. In its place is a bracing, refreshing coolness. The din and dust of the cities is a faint memory, and the terrain has changed slowly from wild jungle to orderly estates where man and nature cooperate. On the lower slopes we pass vast coffee plantations, with occasional jack trees laden with huge fruits. On the higher slopes, coffee gives way to terraced tea gardens dotted with silver firs, whose leaves sparkle in the sunshine. From occasional thatched huts by the roadside I hear the laughter of children and the merry chatter of women. A girl saunters by with a basket on her head, selling mangoes, guavas, and red bananas.

Though there is still a long way to climb, we have gained real mastery of body and mind. During this stage we may be granted a brief glimpse of the summit we are trying to reach. We may free ourselves of severe inhibitions and crippling dependencies. We may find relief from long-standing physical maladies of the heart, lungs, digestive organs, or nervous system, caused by the storm and stress in the mind. Vast reserves of love may be released into our lives, and the capacity to express that love with innate artistry in all relationships. Most of all, our very life becomes a work of art. These are the fruits of sadhana, and we must receive them as they come – without elation, without excitement, without basking in them in any way.

Around a bend in the road we find an unexpected delight: a misty waterfall, formed where countless rivulets merge as they descend. The driver stops for a few minutes so we can have a refreshing drink of this crystal water, flowing among the shrubs and grasses of the slopes like the Ganges high in the Himalayas, which the scriptures say flows down the long, matted locks of Lord Shiva to purify the hearts of his devotees. Teresa of Avila too speaks in this way of divine grace. First, she says, we must draw it all by ourselves from a deep inner well. But the time will come, as she and every sincere aspirant will testify, when grace flows like a steady stream within, giving us strength, determination, and love far beyond our finite means.

Until now we have been making all the effort in our climb. But from now on we feel an unseen power drawing us from above, guarding us against the dangers of the precipitous ascent. This grace does not come from any external power. We have shown our dedication, purified our effort; now the Lord of Love, the Divine Mother within, begins to draw us to her, infusing our limited will with hers, which is infinite.

✳

We are ascending slopes above five thousand feet. The air intoxicates me with its purity; the greens of the foliage and the blue of the sky make me laugh at what I used to call green and blue in the dusty, smoky air of the plains. Even sound has become clearer and purer: the call of a cowherd calling his cows, the song of a wandering *sadhu* chanting the names of the Lord, the laughter of children at play. Just to breathe at these heights is exhilarating. But we need enormous resources to live in this rarefied air – resources we have been developing gradually during our long, arduous ascent from the arid plains to the cool silence of these mountain heights.

We are over six thousand feet now. I hardly feel my body. My mind is still; my ego has been set at rest. The peace in my heart matches the peace at the heart of nature here. This is no strange place. I recognize landmarks, faces, sounds, the shimmer of sunlight on the silver firs far below, the smell of eucalyptus in the pure air. Even the birds and animals are familiar; I seem to know them all.

This is my native state, the state to which I have been striving through the long travail of evolution to return. No longer am I a feverish fragment of life; I am indivisible from the whole. I live completely in the present, released from the prison of the past with its haunting memories and vain regrets, released from the prison of the future with its tantalizing hopes and tormenting fears. All the enormous capacities formerly trapped in past and future flow to me here and now, concentrated in the hollow of my palm. No longer driven by the desire for personal pleasure or profit, I am free to use all these capacities to alleviate the suffering of those around me. In living for others I come to life. "I die," exclaims Saint Paul, "and yet I live: yet not I, but Christ liveth in me."

As I walk up the lane of eucalyptus trees to my home, my heart sings my mantram like a bird at dawn:

> Haré Rama Haré Rama
> Rama Rama Haré Haré
> Haré Krishna Haré Krishna
> Krishna Krishna Haré Haré

Long ago on the plains, with my life filled with the world's daily affairs, I found little time to remember this road, this gate, this cottage where my mother has been waiting. Already it is difficult to remember that there is anything else.

I open the little gate. Mother stands with open arms to receive me. How long has it been? How long have I taken to see through the playthings of the world and come home? *This* is my home. This is everyone's home, where the Divine Mother waits with open arms for all her children to be reunited with her.

I look back beyond the road, where the terraced slopes of the Blue Mountain drop away to the plains so far below. The foothills where I struggled along the noisy, teeming roads are but vague silhouettes; the oppressive plains, where thousands pass the summer without relief, seem no more than a dream. How easy it would be to forget!

But I recall the passengers on the train, the faces of men and women with their work and wares on the road to Coimbatore, the children playing in the noisy bazaar less than a day's journey away. Most of them, I know, seldom think to raise their eyes to the heights we stand on. Few ever dream that this is no inaccessible retreat, but their own home. After absorbing the profound peace of this exalted place, I must go back again to help others turn their eyes upward. Perhaps, when I return here again, I will be able to bring a few home with me.

Glossary

THE SANSKRIT LANGUAGE has several long vowels, which in this glossary are indicated by a bar (‾) over the letter. For practical purposes, the next to the last syllable takes the accent if the vowel is long, but if the vowel is short, then the stress accent falls on the previous syllable, as in Bhā'gavad Gī'tā. Vowels are pronounced as follows: *a* as in *up*, *ā* as in *father*; *i* as in *give*, *ī* as in *see*; *u* as in *put*, *ū* as in *rule*; *e* as in *they*, *ai* as in *aisle*; *o* as in *go*, *au* as in *cow*. All vowels are pronounced; there are no silent letters. The consonants may be pronounced as in English. However, it is helpful to note that Sanskrit makes a distinction between aspirated and unaspirated consonants. For example, there is the consonant *k* pronounced roughly as in the English word *bake*. There is also a *kh*, which is the same sound, with an aspiration or breathing; *kh* is pronounced somewhat like the *k* in *Kate*.

Glossary

ahamkāra The ego-consciousness which makes each person feel separate from all others; inflated sense of self-importance; self-centeredness.

ahimsā Nonviolence, implying an attitude of love for all.

Arjuna A warrior prince who was the companion of Sri KRISHNA in the BHAGAVAD GITA.

āshram [or *āshrama*] A spiritual community; a place where meditation and spiritual disciplines are practiced under a teacher's guidance.

Ātman The Self; the innermost soul in every creature, which is divine.

avatār [or *avatāra*] The incarnation of the Lord on earth. RAMA and KRISHNA are worshipped as avatars in the Hindu tradition; Jesus the Christ and the Compassionate BUDDHA are so regarded also.

Bhāgavad Gītā ["Song of the Lord"] A widely read Hindu scripture which contains the teachings of Sri KRISHNA.

Buddha ["the Awakened One"] Siddhartha Gautama, of the Shakya clan, was known by this title after he attained complete illumination. The Buddha lived and taught in North India from the sixth to the fifth century B.C.

buddhi The discriminating intellect or "higher mind." It functions as a control or guide for the "lower mind," which is directly involved with the demands of the senses.

Dhammapada An important early Buddhist scripture, very appealing in its direct, practical approach.

Gandhi, Mohandas K. (1869–1948) (Called *Mahātma*, "great soul") By bringing ancient spiritual values to bear upon modern situations, Gandhi led India to independence from the British Empire through nonviolence (AHIMSA).

Gītā The BHAGAVAD GITA.

guna Quality; specifically, one of the three qualities that underlie all things: *sattva*, *rajas*, and *tamas* (goodness, passion, and darkness).

Haré The form of the word Hari used in the Haré Rāma MANTRAM. The word *Haré* calls upon *Hari*, the Lord, to bring joy to the mind.

Hinduism The name generally used in the West for India's ancient spiritual tradition. The word comes originally from a Persian word for the people living east of the river Sindhu; Hindus themselves refer to their own religion as *sanātana dharma*, the "eternal law."

karma Literally "action," whether of the body or mind; also the consequences of that action, good or bad, which determine the course of the future. The idea is that every act, word, and thought contains its natural consequences, as a seed may be said to "contain" a tree.

Krishna ["He who draws us to himself"] The historic Krishna is said to have lived in India during the fourteenth century B.C. The mystical Krishna is the Lord of Love who dwells in the hearts of all, a personification of the inner Self or ATMAN.

kundalinī ["the serpent power"] Spiritual or evolutionary energy, which rises through the seven centers of consciousness as spiritual awareness grows.

mahātma ["Great soul"] A loving and respectful title given to many Indian saints and sages, often used in reference to GANDHI.

mantram [or *mantra*] A holy name or phrase; a spiritual formula used to concentrate the mind.

moksha Literally, "liberation" from all mental and spiritual bonds; the final consummation of the spiritual life. Synonymous with NIRVANA.

nirvāna A Hindu and Buddhist term for the final goal of evolution, in which all selfish craving dies and the individual realizes his oneness with all life.

om mani padme hum A Buddhist mantram meaning "the jewel [*mani*] of the Buddha-nature is in the lotus [*padme*] of the heart."

Patanjali Author of the *Yoga Sutras*, a concise description of the way to Self-realization through meditation. He lived in the second century B.C. Though not the first teacher of yoga, he systematized ancient techniques of meditation.

Parvatī ["Daughter of the Mountain"] The Divine Mother, personification of the creative energy of the Godhead, represented as Lord Shiva's beautiful young bride.

Rāma The "Lord of Joy." The historic Rama is regarded as a divine incarnation, like KRISHNA, the Christ, and the Compassionate BUDDHA. In his eternal aspect he represents the Lord within, the Self.

Rāmakrishna (1836–1886) A much-loved saint who lived in Bengal, teaching the validity of all paths to God and bringing renewal to the faiths of India.

Rumi, Jalaluddin A great Muslim mystic and poet in the Sufi tradition, who lived in Asia Minor in the thirteenth century.

sādhana A body of disciplines or way of life which leads to Self-realization. Sadhana is meditation, repetition of the MANTRAM, selfless work, and similar disciplines of the spiritual life.

sādhu A wandering holy man; a sage.

sākshī [Literally "witness"] A name for the Self within, who witnesses all actions but is never involved or tainted by any experience.

samādhi A state of intense concentration in which consciousness is completely unified and a higher mode of knowing unfolds.

samskāra A personality trait conditioned through repeated experiences; a compulsive tendency within the mind which will manifest given the proper environment and stimulus.

Sanskrit The religious and literary language of HINDUISM. Most of the sacred and mystical writings of India are in Sanskrit.

satsang Spiritual fellowship; gathering together with those following the spiritual life.

satyam shivam sundaram A phrase describing God or the supreme reality; literally "truth, joy, beauty."

Shankara ["He who brings about eternal welfare"; a name of SHIVA] A Hindu saint (ca. 780–820) born in Kerala, who is the author of many devotional hymns and important philosophical works.

Shiva God in the aspect of the destroyer, who gives his blessing by putting an end to the ego and to death itself. Shiva is portrayed as the austere cosmic YOGI, eternally rapt in deep meditation.

srī [or *shrī*] A title originally meaning "Lord" or "holy," used today in India as a polite form of address.

Tat [Literally "That"] The divine ground of existence; impersonal, transcendent reality, utterly beyond any kind of description.

Upanishads Ancient Hindu scriptures and earliest of the world's recorded mystical testimonies. They are primarily concerned not with ritual or other aspects of religion, but with Self-realization. The Upanishads form the basis of the Perennial Philosophy in the Indian tradition. In the Katha Upanishad a young seeker learns the secret of the immortal Self from the King of Death. The Shvetashvatara Upanishad is lyrically beautiful, combining devotion to a personal God (the Lord as SHIVA) with the search for Self-realization.

yoga Spiritual union; also a path to Self-realization. Specifically, yoga sometimes refers to the method of meditation and the philosophy taught by PATANJALI.

yogī One who is an adept at meditation (YOGA).

**Blue Mountain
Center of Meditation**

The Blue Mountain Center of Meditation publishes
Eknath Easwaran's books, videos, and audio recordings,
and offers retreats and online programs on his
eight-point program of passage meditation.

For more information and resources, please visit:
www.bmcm.org

The Blue Mountain Center of Meditation
Box 256, Tomales, California 94971 USA
Telephone: +1 707 878 2369
Toll-free in the US: 800 475 2369
Email: info@bmcm.org

CPSIA information can be obtained
at www.ICGtesting.com
Printed in the USA
JSHW020026100821
17709JS00001B/1